CONTEMPORARY IRISH POETRY

CONTEMPORARY IRISH POETRY

edited by

ROBERT GREACEN
& VALENTIN IREMONGER

FABER AND FABER LIMITED
24 Russell Square
London

First published in mcmxlix
by Faber and Faber Limited
24 Russell Square, London, W.C.1
Printed in Great Britain by
Western Printing Services Limited, Bristol

1949

ACKNOWLEDGEMENTS

We wish to thank the authors, publishers and editors who have given permission for poems to be included in this book.

Acknowledgements are due to Mr. Robert Graves for *The Haunted House* from *Collected Poems*; Mr. Daniel Gallen for *Lines on the Death of a Cat* by John Gallen; Messrs. Allen & Unwin, Ltd. for *The Marriage Night* by Austin Clarke; Messrs. William Heinemann, Ltd. for *The False Start, Poem, The Frost Was Hard* and *Two Voyages* by Maurice Craig; Messrs. Reynal & Hitchcock, Inc., New York, for *Pays Conquis* and *Ballad of Mistress Death* by Denis Devlin; Messrs. Jonathan Cape, Ltd. for *Regency Houses, One and One, The Album, The Innocent, Hornpipe* and *Departure in the Dark* by Cecil Day Lewis; and *Afternoon in a Garden at Vinecash, Of Some Compelling Darkness, Where Autumn Poises* and *The Trumpets of Water* by Freda Laughton; The Hogarth Press for *Do Not Expect Again a Phoenix Hour* by Cecil Day Lewis; Messrs. A. D. Peters for *On the Sea Wall* by Cecil Day Lewis; Messrs. George Routledge & Sons Ltd. for *Letter to a Boy in Prison, Epithalamium, In Ireland Now, A Cry* and *The Pattern* by Roy McFadden; Messrs. Frederick Muller Ltd. for *In a Valley of This Restless Mind, The Waterside Poem* and *Vanessa, Vanessa* from *Jubilo* by Ewart Milne; and *The Little Lough, Townland of Peace* and *The Glens* from *No Rebel Word* by John Hewitt; Messrs. W. Tempest, Dundalk, for *Dawn in Inishtrahull* and *Late Evening* from *A Lightkeeper's Lyrics* by D. J. O'Sullivan; Messrs. Martin Secker & Warburg, Ltd. for *An Irish Lake, Stormy Day, Ireland* and *Summer Holiday* by W. R. Rodgers.

Poems are included from the following volumes: *The Hungry Grass* by Donagh MacDonagh (Messrs. Faber & Faber, Ltd.); *Rime, Gentlemen, Please* and *The First Exile* by Robert Farren (Messrs. Sheed & Ward, Ltd.); *The Undying Day* by Robert Greacen (Falcon Press (London) Ltd.); *Always Adam and The Cloth of Flesh* by Sean Jennett (Messrs. Faber & Faber, Ltd.); *Plant and Phantom, The Earth Compels, Springboard* and *Poems* by Louis MacNeice (Messrs. Faber & Faber, Ltd.)

Some of the poems in this anthology first appeared in *The Adelphi, The Bell, The Dublin Magazine, The Irish Times, Life and Letters, Modern Reading, New Road, Outriders, Poetry Folios* and *Voices*.

PREFACE

In selecting the poems for this anthology, we were concerned to show the main trends in contemporary Irish poetry since the publication (in 1928) of Lennox Robinson's *Golden Treasury of Irish Verse*. In particular, our aim has been to present a cross-section of poetry by Irishmen since the death of W. B. Yeats in 1939. Only the work of living poets[1] has been included, the bias being toward the young and less-known: consequently, most of these poems were written either during or after the late war.

In order to establish continuity, however, to give an over-all picture of the contemporary Irish scene, and to indicate more clearly the principal lines of development, poems by certain writers of an older generation have been selected. We wish to point out that Robert Graves, although born in England, is a member of the Graves family of Limerick, where *The Haunted House* was written.

R. G.
V. I.

[1] Captain John Gallen was killed near Poona, India, January 8, 1947, while on active service with the Royal Irish Fusiliers, after we had completed the selection.

CONTENTS

JOHN BOYD

MURLOUGH BAY, 1942

Nothing has changed, no, nothing at all;
northwards Fair Head, bold, perpendicular,
a plumb-line seawards: behold a wall
of grey stone, zigzagging far
across the bay, to farm, field and sheep:
Then a path, white, uncertain,
that if sheep or lamb, lost, should leap
falsely, it is tossed to the curtain
of swaying sea, basalt-bound.
I should keep my peace here, now;
have for company a fierce hound
and a farmer busied with scraping plough.

Nothing seems changed at the lonely farm:
turf still heaped in the draughty shed:
the silent fox still raises loud alarm,
and fowl or lamb soon reckoned dead.
But greeted, news given, I sit by the fire
gossiping to the old patched man,
stiff, grey as rock, brought to lair
here, outrun his life's span.
He recalls all the old wars:
Garibaldi's gamble, the beaten Boers.
In shifting light I stare at scars
and lick the lost century's sores.

Leaving, I look over wall to sea
ruffled by wind stone-cold,
rough as his handshake after tea,

grey as fine sepulchral mould.
The wind shakes my cottage door:
the kitchen is cold, table white as bone.
Through one pane the rounded rocks of Tor
paw seawards, splashed with foam.
A cowl-like mist covers Fair Head:
falls softly, leaving one sharp shoulder.
I turn from the window to face the red
glow of turf: shadows grow bolder.
I could keep my peace here, now,
with shy seal and silent sheep,
if only these teeming times would allow
the salve of silence and of sleep.

TOWARDS DONEGAL

The halo of sun now holds the hills
of Donegal, while here I stand
watching the gathering cloud that falls
over those hills nightly, like a fan
unfolded in an orient tale.
I have never known those lost hills
nor their people; nor the soft tongue
spoken there; nor the silence that falls
with the soldered sun; nor the valleys along
the crackling coast now bare of sail
or smoke of ship. Yet I can tell
my children legends woven there
in winter's woe: and telling feel
the spell in the wondering stare
of candid eyes captured by the living tale.

G. M. BRADY

THE WOOD

Within the picnic-haunted wood,
Beneath the deep bough's loss of green and light,
Lovers, from sullen Sunday streets released,
Lie whispering, entranced, upon their bed,
Heedless of season's rout about their ears,
While birds cry, challenging the gales
That are obedient to Time's urgent law.

Call rook, scream gull, darken the sky
With hooded messengers of future wrath,
Their arms defend against all threats
The heart's terrain, although others fly,
Although warring storms defeat the course
Of sunlight and rivers, chilling their flow,
And hurries fugitive the orphaned leaf.

But when the lark sings to the sun
Above the shawl of corn across its hill,
And every tree shakes green its sheltering cave,
When roads are dust-drowsed and the rivers run
Under cool bridges, what shall have endured?
O, Lovers, be absolute, make your world strong
Against the sky's anger. Winter is long.

THE RESTLESS MEN

Fever of unrest led them to the water,
Men whom the lean land mothered without love,
Led them in silence, famine's cloud above them,
Far from the stony acres of their homes.

Far from the shelterless, unfriendly tree,
From where a shawl of shadow hid grief's stare,
The valleys autumn entered like a thief,
As the last bird sang to the flooding fall.

But when the smell of terror chilled their lungs
A numb voice spoke. Was this the sea
For which hearths were deserted and the fields
Left to the throttling rule of weed and briar?

Was this the sea, the road that was to lead
To valleys calm and rich to eye and ear,
Green wealth and wells? Did we for this
Leave our children hungry, our women without fire?

No voice replied, warning through winds that lurched
Across the harbour dark with straining ships,
As their eyes lifted and each intent face
Searched for an answer in the gull-wild sky.

Yet many went who heard beyond the storm
The siren islands calling, heard the words,
Faint but enticing through gull's scream of want,
Promising affluence to the restless heart,

Went, but in silence now return, men whom
The myth abandoned to a wilderness.
While those whose blood lost fever in wild water
Swing languidly, deep in the blameless seas.

NOCTURNE

Across the square, across the lake lights glow,
And echoing through sour alley-ways the engines
fade

Into the rustling air, a stillness holds, until
The clock-towers storm each other's pinnacles,
Deafening the chapel quiet of hours
That softly, sandal-shod, behind chained doors
Walk the dust's sanctuary until daylight strikes.

The wind stirs, down the tall street slinks,
Edging along the railings, stealthy as those
Who move from lamp to lamp, the outcast ones,
The hungry and the haunted wanderers
Passing like ghosts by curtained houses where
Side to warm side the sleepers also are
Lost in fear's maze, stranded on shores as dark.

Night settles on the statue in the square
A lonelier pose of anonymity.
Far, far away, a light goes out.
Room above room, stranger by stranger laid,
At last weary of streets some go to bed.
Over their city, monuments and lanes,
Stars wheel, and locked again in night's small cell
The prisoner stares at the agonizing wall.

Dust drifts across the creaking floor,
Breathing through keyholes, gathering in the hall
Where Silence, close-lipped as a gossip, leans
An eavesdropping shadow on the sombre door.

AUSTIN CLARKE

THE STRAYING STUDENT

On a day when sails were blowing southward,
A bishop sang the Mass at Inishmore,
Men took one side, their wives were on the other
But I heard the woman coming from the shore:
And wild in despair my parents cried aloud
When they saw the vision draw me to the doorway.

Long had she lived in Rome when Popes were bad,
The wealth of every age she makes her own,
Yet smiled on me in eager admiration,
And for a summer taught me all I know,
Banishing shame with her great laugh that rang
As if a pillar caught it back alone.

I learned the prouder counsel of her throat.
My mind was growing bold as light in Greece;
And when in sleep her limbs were shown,
I blessed the noonday rock that knew no tree:
And for an hour the mountain was her throne,
Although her eyes were bright with mockery.

They say I was sent back from Salamanca
And failed in logic, but I wrote her praise
Nine times upon a college wall in France.
She laid her hand at darkfall on my page
That I might read the heavens in a glance
And I knew every star the Moors have named.

Awake or in my sleep, I have no peace now,
Before the ball has struck, my breath has gone,

And yet I tremble lest she may deceive me
And leave me in this land, where every woman's son
Must carry his own coffin and believe,
In dread, all that the clergy teach the young.

THE LUCKY COIN

Collect the silver on a Sunday,
Weigh the pennies of the poor,
His soul can make a man afraid
And yet thought will endure.
But who can find by any chance
A coin of different shape
That never came from Salamanca
Or danced on chapel plate?

Though time is slipping through all fingers
And body dare not stay,
That lucky coin, I heard men tell it,
Had glittered once in Galway
And crowds were elbowing the spirit
While every counter shone,
Forgetting grief until the ages
Had changed it for a song.

Turning in cartwheels on the fairground,
The sun was hastier—
That strolling girls might have for dowry.
Two hands about a waist;
Men voted for the Liberator
After the booths were closed
And only those in failing health
Remembered their own souls.

On Nephin many a knot was tied,
The sweet in tongue made free there,
Lovers forgot on the mountain-side
The stern law of the clergy
That kiss, pinch, squeeze, hug, smack denied,
Forgot the evil, harm
And scandal that come closer, lying
In one another's arms.

Not one of us will ever find
That coin of different shape
For it was lost before our rising
Or stolen—as some say.
But when our dread of the unseen
Has rifled hole and corner,
How shall we praise the men that freed us
From everything but thought.

TENEBRAE

This is the hour that we must mourn
With tallows on the black triangle,
Night has a napkin deep in fold
To keep the cup; yet who dare pray
If all in reason should be lost,
The agony of man betrayed
At every station of the cross?

O when the forehead is too young,
Those centuries of mortal anguish,
Dabbed by a consecrated thumb
That crumbles into dust, will bring
Despair with all that we can know;
And there is nothing left to sing,
Remembering our innocence.

I hammer on that common door,
Too frantic in my superstition,
Transfix with nails that I have broken,
The angry notice of the mind.
Close as the thought that suffers him,
The habit every man in time
Must wear beneath his iron shirt.

An open mind disturbs the soul,
And in disdain I turn my back
Upon the sun that makes a show
Of half the world, yet still deny
The pain that lives within the past,
The flame sinking upon the spike,
Darkness that man must dread at last.

THE MARRIAGE NIGHT

O let her name be told
At dusk—while fishermen
Take nobles on the oar
And pass the fiery dice
Of wineshops at the harbour,
That flush them in the haze:
There is a darker town
Of ships upon the wave.

The morning she rode down
Where topsails, that had brought
A blessing from the Pope,
Were scrolled in early water:
Such light was on her cheekbone
And chin—who would not praise
In holy courts of Europe
The wonder of our days?

All saw in that cathedral
The great Earls kneel with her;
The open book was carried,
They got up at the gospel.
In joy the clergy prayed,
The white-clad acolytes
Were chaining, and unchaining,
Fire-hearted frankincense.

Upon her night of marriage,
Confessions were devout;
Murmuring, as religion
Flamed by, men saw her brow.
The Spaniards rolled with flag
And drums in quick relays;
Our nobles were encamping
Each day around Kinsale.

But in deceit of smoke
And fire, the spoilers came:
Tower and unmortar'd wall broke
Rich flight to street and gate.
O she has curbed her bright head
Upon the chancel rail
With shame, and by her side
Those heretics have lain.

RHODA COGHILL

IN WICKLOW

The high trees grieve like the sea's water.
The sad sky crouches on Carraig and Slaughter;
And a crude donkey, in the windy quarter
    Calls up the rain.
Sunlight sleeps in the tinker's kettle,
Where twilight-bannered, elfin nettle
And the fool's-parsley's starry clusters battle
    For kingship of the lane.

Clouded waves comb the shadowed shore,
Sifting the sliding shingle for
What, in past time, furnished the sea's floor,
    Seaweed or stone;
And the old gypsy gropes, to find,
Thrown on the foreshore of her mind,
Forgotten things, washed up and left behind,—
    Thoughts that were once her own.

BURREN, Co. CLARE

For Luba Kaftannikoff

Here have I drifted on a quiet wave
Of happening, that gently washes
Where Time's slow-flowing ocean flood has
  shaped
Age-old valley and hill.
Its waters, lapping still
About me in imagination, have

Confused my sense: so birds like fishes
Swim in the liquid air, and lichened bushes
Have turned to branching coral the sheep on
the mountain-side
To flecks of foam left by an ebbing tide.

Forgotten, solitary,
The casual flotsam of an epoch I,
Where crumbling mortuary mounds
Of ancient men are found,
Who lie, long buried, leagues below
The cyclic ebb and flow
Of Time's refashioning,—drowned
Beneath slow tide on tide of history.

MAURICE CRAIG

THE FALSE START

Ask it now, if you will, of those who stand
On balconies for the first time in the year,
Ask how they take the tentative approach
Of idle airs that coax the trees to bud
Gently and suddenly, across the road.

Some will confess to blood's uneasiness
At finding the year's curve deflected up
Abruptly, tasting shyly like a beast
The unfamiliar stimulus, each sense
Sharp with suspicion.

Others may let pass
(Being so regularly ground and wound
That nothing strange disturbs them) these
mild skies,
The sweetness and the slightness of these
winds,
With some stale stock remark that
scarcely wakes
The lightly-sleeping echo, lulled so long.

And some remain in whom the lost response
Is found and reinfused by conscious thought.
Double distrust restricts each breath they take:
The frost's behind them; and the frost in front
Threatens the shoots they watch, the shoots that
push
Their tender spearheads in the long-tilled field,

Bright-pointed thoughts that spring so quick, so
bright
That eyes that look direct see only sun.

Anticipation, retrospect, alone
Can dwell upon the lucid interval.
We lack the lithe resilience of the boughs
That bear the flowering blossom to the breeze.
The warmth and liquefaction of our earth
Dissolve, as well, the sense that should respond,
As though the instant blurred our eyes with tears
And clarity of sight could only come
Before they flow, or after they have dried.

POEM

Salt of the bitten lip
Smudges the world with tears:
That inland breath may keep
The sad smell of the sea,
To each unlocking mouth
That could not taste itself
The convoluting shell
Brings winds from west and south.

Salt of the sprawling weed
Lingers upon the tongue
Though eyelids cracked and red
Save soft eyes from the sun
That warms the fields of corn.
Tears that are shed by fools
Flood, and we still renew
Though land and weed may burn.

Shell with shell fits; our lives
Sprawl, but we tell the story
That only two such halves
Fit, as were one before.
—An idiot, wandering in sleep
Picked them up once; who knows
How many exactly so
Still crawl where salt is cheap?

THE FROST WAS HARD

The frost was hard those days, the sunlight clean
Each morning on the snow, and every night
Our footsteps rang like iron on the road
As, walking homeward through the misty air
We kept the mist of breath about us. You
Remember still, thawing the frozen pipes
With cans of boiling water?

To be sure
That frost was hard for you and me; but now
The long sobs of the dying afternoon
Are caught and choked in autumn's throat. The
leaves
Made fools of by the black heart of the wind
Skelter along the pathways. In the west
The flickering furnace glows more cold, and there
Beyond the mountains desolately stretch
The bitter marshes under the empty sky.

Where can we find the water now, to thaw
These frozen seas of blood, that superfused
With blood fresh-flowing, congeal about the heart?
The generous impulse in the arteries

That circulate between us has not flagged
On either side. For that and all it means
My gratitude is inarticulate
And best employed to keep those channels free
Through all the darkness of this winter night.

BALLAD TO A TRADITIONAL REFRAIN

Red brick in the suburbs, white horse on the wall,
Eyetalian marbles in the City Hall:
O stranger from England, why stand so aghast?
May the Lord in His mercy be kind to Belfast.

This jewel that houses our hopes and our fears
Was knocked up from the swamp in the last
hundred years;
But the last shall be first and the first shall be last:
May the Lord in His mercy be kind to Belfast.

We swore by King William there'd never be seen
An All-Irish Parliament at College Green,
So at Stormont we're nailing the flag to the mast:
May the Lord in His mercy be kind to Belfast.

O the bricks they will bleed and the rain it
will weep,
And the damp Lagan fog lull the city to sleep;
It's to hell with the future and live on the past:
May the Lord in His mercy be kind to Belfast.

TWO VOYAGES

I. SUMMER

Leaving the bar slack-watered, I have left
The quiet man in the corner with his pint
Who did not speak, the hour
We drank and chatted there.

High walls of granite over-arched with elder
Dividing gardens. Long deserted lanes
Behind the houses. Here
The cats walk warily.

I walk with them to you, who like a cat
Sit curled and purr before an empty grate.
Two points of light have hailed
Each other in the night.

II. WINTER

Love's equinoctial gales are past, the path
Along the long lanes leads again through night.
The trees are bare, the air
A halo round each lamp.

Gentlest imaginable groundswell heaving
Hardly disturbs the wrack. The wave that broke
Over us both, has passed
And now the calm succeeds.

And now the fire's the focus of the room—
By winter made so. Like a gay salute
There crackles in the hearth
The holly's fusillade.

LESLIE DAIKEN

BINOCULARS ON WEST CORK

Daily and infallibly as the changing of the moon
The tidal estuary creeps coaxingly into the fjord
Between the grazed thighs of the promontories
Like a happy lover slipping into welcome sheets.

It subsides to the fluted cries of waterfowl and waders
Uncovering mousegrey mudflats and the unashamed ribs
Of ageold hulks. Daily and infallibly, the tide.

•

What broken tower can we hide in the day after
to-morrow?
What hulk launch when all our argosies have foundered?
The tide of a battle in which we feel too aloof to bleed,
The pressure of its tense desire upon the mud-flats of
Our manias: these will submerge us, nibbling away
Our fantasies, ripping the timbers of our unconcern
With the unappeasable fury of the ocean.

And when the seagrass has hidden altogether the
desolate
Stones of our jetties: when the curlew and the kittiwake
Have withdrawn even their patronage from the seething
mud,
A day will break over the twin knuckles of the forelands,
Teasling the clouds with geranium, the water with rust,
And a vessel from Asia Minor, a mongol skipper in her
prow,
Map in his hand, statistics throbbing in his head,

Will bring another ethic to this island, wherein the
Norseman's avarice and Saxon's lure and fine Phoenician's
craft
Will sink into the immemorial mud like a ship's hulk,
Picked out of being by carnivorous waters.

LINES WRITTEN IN A COUNTRY PARSON'S ORCHARD

This stock whom Cromwell planted here,
Tough seedlings of efficiency,
Has walled its acres in, from fear,
Founded a generous dynasty.

His plea with God, his door ajar,
The Rector listens to the rooks;
Puzzling the scourge of total war
Clings to his fishing-rods and books.

And so, the Mistress of the House,
Her servants mortgaged to the times,
Now weeds and plants, her haughty grouse
Hushed by the apple-trees and limes.

And if the Mistress' back is bent,
Her heart is broken from the knowledge
That all her psalms and thrift have meant
Sweet nothing to her son at College.

In raffia gardening-hat, and gloves,
Godly as one of Millet's *Gleaners*,
Stooping, she sighs because she loves
The youth despite his misdemeanours.

Each week her pleas oppress the lad:
'Oh, make Dean Swift your inspiration . . .
She disremembers Swift went mad
Before his genius shocked the nation.

Unanswered every one. The boy,
Pursuing an evasive Venus,
Is amorous, matricidal, coy—
A nineteen-year-old blond Adonis.

Impatient of the rustic Church,
His bibles all are secular:
Should Mary leave him in the lurch
He'll follow his integral star,

And, poet of the mouldering home,
He still will live to sing and see
How little reaped where they had sown-
The generous Ascendancy.

DENIS DEVLIN

PAYS CONQUIS

The invader came again and conquered
With the old by-product crimes
But three years later the harvest flaunted,
The young kept faith with time.
The invader built bridges, roads
Feeding the pastures to the ports;
Endowed schools where experts learned
To drain the steam rebellion churned.
The mayor, the general forgot
Jean and Jacques unjustly shot.

And when the careless earth brought forth
Well-fed children, wheat and coal
More than the laws provided for:
The shadowy experts muffed their role;
Jacques in his widow's bed was hate,
The rifles hid by Jean were bared
To win back pride in free estate;
And refuse papers flew in the square
Outside the scared Proconsulate.

BALLAD OF MISTRESS DEATH

'Oh, I've had ten men before you',
Said my redhead Sally;
'Yes, and a hundred men before you',
Said my new-found darling.
The sea's blue maw glittered

Like a fat, barbaric queen's,
And her thighs were white and gold
Like wisp-rain in sunshine.

In the long hall with statues
We sat and were not lonely,
Her name all forgotten,
My darkhead, my darling
Said in a gentle voice:
'And you never will be jealous
Though many's the man's head
Has lain upon my pillow,
For you've found out my secret
And many's the man more will.'

'Yes, I've found out your secret',
Said I to my darling,
Walking the dark streets
Through leaf-shaken lamplight.
'I never will be jealous
Nor you numb or nag at me
I'll name you the world's most beauty
Yellowheaded Helen
And no lie be telling;
No woman will disprove it.'

She held me like nightfall
Her breath came like knives
While the housing plains sank lower
With their cinder-grates of cities—
Oh, there will need no porters
When all those doors open!

PADRAIC FALLON

THE WAISTCOAT

Oro, the islandmen
Load herring from the white shoals
Into the barrows of the shawled fishwives
On the grey wall of Galway:
And lightly where sunlight was warehoused
  by the water
From the tarred hulls they sway
In their blue homespuns and skin shoes
To the hazy wall and away.

O tell me what lazy Peeler
Thumbing his girth will dare them
Now money that ripens like rain on ropes
Runs down their hasty fingers?
And what fat terrified son of the devil
That tends a till won't pull black porter
All night for men whose eyes make knives
Of the lights that worm through his bottled
  windows?

But quietly at last as a sheep-fair
From the old square the day disperses,
One spark of the sun stands hitched
Like a lonely ram in a corner,
And Padraic the son of Patcheen Rua
Shakes the drink from the wild top of his skull
And stoops from the door in his whispering shoes
To dandle the sky on his shoulder.

O grey city
Of stone and mist and water,
Here's terror, a son of Clan Flaherty
Footloose in your sleepy air.
Have you no shocked sudden memory
Of rape and ringing steeple
As he grows in a lane, towering, till the sea
Seems no more size than a mackerel?

Fly for the bishop, quick.
Call all the lazy constables for, O,
By Padraic Patcheen Rua now
An innocent woman idles.
Bright in the midnight of her shawl
Her face rises, in her own light
Her piled hair slipping from the comb
Could hide a lover out of sight.

O, Padraic Patcheen Rua, such a woman
Never had a match
In any thatched house on the windy island;
And, O, Padraic, did she stretch
On the top of a headland with you of an
  evening
What riches your great hand would win
Burning on all her slow horizons down
From crown to shin.

Man dear, do you dawdle
And the world before you?
A ship with two sails
And a gallow's crew,
And the wind right for Connemara
Where you can have your will
And Potheen in a jug
By a three-legged stool?

Open your mouth, O dolt.
Strike the great silver string.
Give the gossips a story, we sicken
Of talking of tides and fish.
Lay hands on her, show her the rocks
And rainbows of water we twist
Out of ourselves for the women, bringing
An ocean on the bowsprit.

Are you making a mock of us, Padraic?
Is an islandman backing
Round like a colt if a woman
But finger his elbow?
By God, do you turn and run
And she trying to hold you
So hard that you leave in her two hands
Three parts of your woollen waistcoat?

O, your wife will magnify you
To our wives at the chapel door.
And a hundred and twenty-seven saints whose
bones
Are green grass in Killeaney
Will praise you with faces flashing on the eaves
Of heaven like wintry drops of rain.
But what of us, Padraic, what of us,
Men raised to the sea?

What of the men who tie the wind in ropes
And lead the sea horses by little bridles?
What of us who catch fish
In shudders of black starlight?
What will the noisy fishwomen cry from the wall
As we creep out towards the sky?
Ah, Padraic, I who tell the story
Cover my face and sigh.

RAFTERY'S DIALOGUE WITH THE WHISKEY

RAFTERY

If you shortened many a road and put a halo
On every thought that was growing in my head,
Have I not been to you as the brown nut to the hazel,
Your fruit, O my comrade?
And in many a lonely bed have I not praised you
With sleepy words no virgin ever heard?
And after all this, O the spite of it, here in Kilchreest
You topple a tallow candle and burn my beard.

Troy in its tall sticks never burned with a blaze
As bright as Raftery's hairs when that evil spark
Leaped on his skull and from that holy rooftree
Pitchforked his spluttering thatch;
Shame on you! not even Mercury who rose
Out of the cradle to fall on evil ways,
Stealing cattle, would hobble my wits and roast them
Hide and hair like that in the fire of my face.

O I was the sight then and the great commotion;
Wells running dry and poor people peeling their legs
With barrels and pails, and the fish flying down to
the ocean;
And look at me now! a mere plaster of white of eggs!
Look at me! A bonfire to folly! but no man
Was ever saint till he was a sinner first;
And I'll break with you now though it cost me the
mannerly company
Of the gay talkers who follow a thirst.

So I dismiss you. Here! Take your mouth from my
mouth!
I have weighed you, O creature of air, and the weigh-
man cries,

'Here's nothing will balance a holding of land in the
south,
Beef on the hoof there and grass climbing up to
the skies;
What's whiskey to hanging bacon?
To a glittering hearth and blue delphware?
Will it put a Sunday coat on any man,
I ask you, or leave him to walk bare?'

Ah, sweet whisperer, my dear wanton, I
Have followed you, shawled in your warmth, since I
left the breast,
Been toady for you and pet bully,
And a woeful heartscald to the parish priest;
And look! If I took the mint by storm and spent it,
Heaping on you in one wild night the dazzle of a
king's whore,
And returned next morning with no money for a curer,
Your Publican would throw me out of the door.

THE WHISKEY

You blow hot and cold, grumbling,
The privilege of the woman and the poet.
Now let me advise you, Man of the fancy stomach,
Carry a can and milk a nanny goat!
Drink milk! for I am not for you—as I am not indeed
For your brother the miser; but, ah, when the miser's
heir
Grows into manhood and squanders I'll walk through
the company
And call that man my dear.

I grow too heady now for your grey blood;
And you do little good to my reputation
With your knock-knees and tremulous jowls—for
God's sake

Pay the tailor to press your pelt and tuck it in!
What can I be to you now but a young wife to an old man?
Leave me to the roarers in the great universities,
The masters of Latin with the big ferules
Who know what use strong whiskey is!

Hush, now! I'll speak or burst. You have no pith,
And I pity the botch of a carpenter who planed you down.
You are maudlin at table ere the company is lit,
And among clowns, the heaviest clown.
I have given you pleasure, yet you round on me like a lackey
Who will swear he was overworked and underpaid;
And to-morrow, O most grievous insult of all, you'll repent of me
That the priest may help you into a holy grave.

RAFTERY

Ah, that tongue was sharpened in many a bad house
Where candles are hooded on the black quays of the world;
Many is the sailor it stripped to the bleak hose
And the Light Dragoon with his feather furled;
I hear it now and I pray that a great bishop
Will rise with a golden crook and rout you out of the land,
Yourself and the rising family of your sins,
As Patrick drove the worms out of Ireland.

You're an illness, a cancer, a canker, a poison,
Galloping consumption, broken breath,
Indiaman's liver, thin diseases of the person,
Cholera Morbus and the yellow death;

You're the two sour women who wait here by my
 mattress
With Christian charity and broken hen-eggs
To mess my only features, but if I live to denounce you
I'll empty every tavern when I get upon my legs.

THE WHISKEY
If hard words broke bones every sad rascal
With a bleached tongue who turns on me of a morning
Would have done for me long ago, yet I rise again like
 the pasch
Quietly, brightly, in their minds and they return.

RAFTERY
Who returns but the shiftless drifters, the moon's men?
Stray calves who'd suck at any udder?
Waifs, bagmen, beggars, and an odd fool of a lord
Crazy enough not to know better?

THE WHISKEY
Men of merriment, the wide girthed men
Whose eyes pen cattle, and slender men who hold
The curves of a filly together with one finger
While the other strips an heiress of her gold;
Equal those, O Fiddler, men of the great gay world
Who can dance a stately figure or bow prettily to a
 queen
And keep fine manners though the blood be rearing
Like a red stallion on the fair green.

RAFTERY
Blackguards, rakes, who rise up from cards
Only when the sun is trumped there on the table
Like the red ace of hearts, take them, the gamblers
Who wouldn't pay their debts were they able;
Dicers, procurers, who'll give you an I.O.U.

On the honour or dishonour of a wife or daughter,
Take them, the lot of them, hog, devil, or dog,
And drown them in a bucket of bog water.

THE WHISKEY
Poets and musicians——

RAFTERY
and absentee landlords,
Militiamen on hayfeet—strawfeet who burn
Brightly as red lamps in a lanewife's back parlour,
Taking, as always, the wrong turn;
I leave you to them and to the landlord's agent
Who shivers beside you day-in day-out
Walled in by the hostile murmurs of the rainy grass-lands
In an old windy house.

THE WHISKEY
For a homespun poet whose pride I nursed
When doors were shut on him and dogs barked at his heels,
Your gratitude is such I'll swear a cutpurse was your father
And your mother the lady who tied eels.
Desert me, indeed? You windy bag of old words,
You wan wizened weasel with one worn tooth!
If I whistled to-morrow you'd hobble to me on your sores;
And that's the truth.

RAFTERY
Whistle, then!

THE WHISKEY
I'll whistle when
I'm in the mood.

Raftery

Whistle! Whistle!

The Whiskey

Maybe when you've money and can spend,
When you're a farmer slaughtering the poor thistle,
Stoning crows or coaxing cows,
Counting your corn grain by grain,
With thirteen bonhams to every one of your sows,
And you carrying a big purse at the fair.

Raftery

Good-bye for ever then!

The Whiskey

Good-bye, Raftery.

Raftery

I'll never be a farmer.

The Whiskey

And where is the need?
Poetry and whiskey have lived always on the country.
Why wouldn't they indeed?

Raftery

You're right. Why shouldn't I tax the heavy farmer?
I give him wit. And you? You give him—what?

The Whiskey

No matter. We are two necessary luxuries.

Raftery

Listen! I'll drink to that.

MAURICE FARLEY

THE HELL-FIRE CLUB

Our ghosts still walk upon the mountain top,
And the grey walls still rise upon that height
Up whose steep slopes we drove so long ago,
In our wild passage putting peace to flight.

Perhaps about those ruins yet there clings
The wicked splendour of our memories—
Nights when we supped with Satan, and the stars
Grew pale above our mounting revelries.

Above the sleeping city where we met
The night was riven by strange melody.
The fall of dice, the clinking glass, and oft
The clash of steel, made bitter threnody.

Strange guests were gathered round our board—
  Ill-fame
And Death, and one more sinister than they,
Who entered with the midnight to the feast,
And in the dawn, none marking, slipped away.

Or ever where he sat the play ran high,
And in the flush of wine no man kept ward:
From the quick word the quicker quarrel rose,
And swords were measured on the moonlit sward.

But when his chair was empty, and the beams
Of morning through the shutters palely shone,
That old reveller, Night, flung down his cards,
Drew his dark cloak around him—and was gone.

Still we played on, or with uncertain hands,
Filled up to drink defiance to the day,
Yet as it brightened so our spirits waned,
And one and all at last made haste away.

'Spur on the horses'—as we rattle past
From dewy fields the startled cattle gaze
At us askance. Then, as the sound of wheels
Grows faint, forget us and return to graze.

A roofless ruin now our meeting-house
The straying cow with gentle lowing fills,
And the long peace we shattered for an hour
Now reigns again upon the quiet hills.

SOLILOQUY IN SAINT PATRICK'S

I feel the darkness near—my living death,
That all my powers can now no longer brave.
Let me then write my challenge while 'tis hot,
And fling my gage into the coming grave.

For here, amid the cloisters and the dead,
Freed from the bondage of the flesh and bone,
I'll come to rest, perhaps. Then overhead
I'll set my last defiance, carved in stone.

'Burning with indignation'—ah! that pain
Was not all born of my own thwarted pride:
Nor could it, coming from so small a source,
Embrace a catalogue of wrongs so wide.

Easy for him who knows no care beyond
His own small want, and lacks no part of it,
To live indifferent to a needier world,
And cavil at the vitriol of my wit.

Better the burning heart, the restless brain,
Than to be born without the power to feel
The woes of man, to lack the driving force
To forge in hopeless cause the barbs of steel.

But 'twas not always battle. Youth and charm
Could find me worthy of Vanessa's day.
Old women in the market called me friend.
And what of tenderness?—Let Stella say.

But love can come no further, and no strife
Will more be fanned to fury by my breath;
For there awaits me soon the long turmoil,
Whose only ease is in the thought of death.

And past the grave? What do I hope to find?
What hangs before me like a Golden Fleece—
The last emollient of the torn mind—
In life denied me—an eternal peace.

Then they who filched away a people's rights,
Finding how poor a watch their enemy keeps,
Will coin for me a briefer epitaph,
And say 'Thank God—at last the Drapier sleeps'.

SECOND THOUGHTS

I thought you offered me a summer's day,
The passing pleasure of an idle hour.
My heart rejected what was scarcely said,
Before it burst, responsive, into flower.

Why is the mind so slow to leave the past?
Why will the heart to ancient madness cling?

Now that the die is cast, the chance refused,
I know you offered me another spring.

Another spring! an hour of youth and bliss,
With all its promise, all its hope, renewed,
Like that I sacrificed to other gods,
And doubly dear, because so soon eschewed.

Your words have touched to life a barren tree,
And left, beyond regrets or gratitude,
A second bloom of youth and energy,
That winter's hand can never quite denude.

ROBERT FARREN

RIME, GENTLEMEN, PLEASE

The Poets, at Tailteann drouthy, and drouthy at Tara,
favoured jorums of the heather-juice, the mead.
The poets, after Saint Patrick, took them to draughting
the brooks and the spring wells in their own fields.
Norse skalds conveyed the wind that shakes the barley,
brewing the poets ale of their own sheaves.
While Normans shipped the claret in Ormond's barrels
when Galway proffered port to courts and seas.

O Carolan wetted his whistle after his harping
with a glass that was like water, tintless, clear,
though it leaped the lip and skidded the tongue more
sharply,
and lit his ending world with morning's gleam.
The bungs are out from Seán O Tuama's barrels,
and Seán sees port like Homer's 'wine-dark seas'
go pouring down the poets' open hatches
and roll the poets round like wrecked triremes.

So, poets from the foothills and the ledgers,
lively around the white wines and the red,
the screw that plies the bottles for you dredges
the silt of years and grapples the foundered dead
You, heir to Alighieri's face, sip sherry:
over you, by the hundred traceless heads
of the men that lilted the heart of Ireland merry,
the silkfine songs of 'Spanish wine' are said

Behind you, man swivelling a wrist and ferrying
your whiskey down and whispering 'Catullus said——'
O Carolan's swivelling his harper's wrist, and ferrying,
and hurrying with harper's fingers Catullus' tread.
There's Donncha Rua Mac Namara looming
by the man who made his fame a trilogy's.
And Raftery, fuddle-pated by the bouquets,
sighs 'Pockets must have filled since I lacked sprees'.

Among the living men a man is proving
no one translated Rahilly only he;
but through the fast-shut door a soul is moving:
'Long ago,' lips Rahilly, 'Death translated me.'
'And Death translated me and my translator',
comes from the bittern's mourner, Cahal Bwee,
'then he bustled the blackbird boy, was the third lamenter,
up onto the Heavenly Plain, by the way 'twas Meath.'

[O yellow bittern, yours was a brilliant ending;
it bound in a ghostly friendship three like these:
your corpse on the ice took the eyes of three good verse-
men;
the last is a dust by the side of the Grecian seas.
Whisper! Old Cahal Bwee Mac Gilla Gunna
turns lovely mourning for your drouthy throat;
Ledwidge renames you, keening for Tom MacDonagh
who keyed the mourning to another note.]

Now Cahal Bwee's long dead who made strong music;
Thomas MacDonagh's dead, who made it new;
Ledwidge, the blackbird, drowned in the loud bugles. . . .
Ghosts of these poets come and go with you—
son to the one and heir to the three dead men—
under your lowest murmur murmuring 'we
bid you end quick-limed song, and song whose ending
drowned in the battle-horns by the Greek sea'.

Look, through the live men's talk and the dead's miming
another poet's ghost comes lumberingly,
one who's still body-clumsy and clogged with writhing
rhythms unpurged before the soul shot free.
Listen: 'No poet here has seen this wonder.
O if he could only bear it, being alive,
my soul would flow above his ear and murmur,
"So . . . it was shown me since the day I died." '

Poets that come from foothills and from ledgers,
poets rooted in grasslands and in stones,
singer whose father sang and foretold terrors,
and riming men looted of eyes and bones—
here where the glass tilts and the lip pouches
and the coin chinks through the dribbled, lancing words,
I, with a written verse and a glass, salute you:
spirits, and living men, with the mouths of birds.

From 'THE FIRST EXILE'

The King Threatens the Poets

I will drive them,' King Ae Mac Ainmirë
hammered like a smithy tune,
'from the cummers and the courts of Ireland,
from the flock-bed of lios and dún.
I will harry them plunging in the currachs
from the three frothy waves of the west,
and scuttle them in Gaulish marshes
and then there'll be kings'll have rest.

'And then there'll be kings'll keep satin
brought hardly through blast and through hail;
their wives'll wear jewels at the wrestling
and not give them up at the tale.

There'll be peace! There'll be peace! There'll be
knowing
your cloak'll stay snug on your back
and your tunic not loosen its loopcord
when greed-mothered rime makes a clack.

'I will drive them from the cummers and the
copses,
I will run them, for black Fomors, to the ships.
Then I'll clash my cup on any cup in Tara,
The kings of every airt'll shell their lips,
and the shout come running from them like the
sea-drone
or the bursting of wavewind through shelly sand:
"They are gone! Almighty God bring never
homeward
the louts half-rimed us out of house and land."'

SLEEP

While now I lay me down to sleep
I pray to God my soul to keep,
that, riding out with sleep to-night,
it may turn back with morning's light.

Or, if in sleep it slip my clay,
may it blaze back to that High Day
it left behind to make me man
out of the thing that flesh began. . . .

Though flesh and flesh together go
and man beget and woman grow,
yet is there nothing human made
till the new spirit start its trade.

Aye, flesh can sow in flesh, and can
raise crop, but not the crop of man:
until the down-sent soul is come
no human hand or head's begun;
until the ripeness feel the soul
entice it to contrive man-bone
the passion-sown, womb-stemming plant,
bid to turn human, cannot start;
and God makes freshly each new soul
God, the all-making God, alone.

Then, ghostly-begun by Holy Ghost,
soul to its groping man-thing gropes
and soul and thing make man. Man, born,
walks the wild, haunted world in storm,
in head's and heart's and hand's bright force;
till head, heart, hand each failing goes
earth under haunted earth to turn
down being's steps to stem and worm.
But back the perpetual soul, impelled,
hurtles to Christ, the Lustrous Head.

There then's the map, the world's design
which all forms fit—man, sleep and time.

By hand's and heart's and head's bright force
the living man through earth's life goes;
but force of hand in soul begins,
and souls have force beyond hearts' brims;
so, thought for wing, soul levitates
loose of limbs' plot of time and space;
it beats light wings through time that was
it spans the silken seas of God,
it tips the aevum's endless start,
eternity's live, stirless heart.

Soul can contrive a thought like God's,
body its thought in verse or bronze,
rib it, add limb—of note, of stone—
just as God gives clay limb to soul:
old thing into unknown thing turned
soul can exalt, expand, the world.

And yet, with this high-searching soul,
man has the death-drift in the bone.
Man's spirit (breath of body's breath,
still heart of beating heart, fine weft
of fleshly weave), alive in sense,
sups on the sensuous universe.
It fans the fiery, clay-blood heart,
drifts with the senses' drift to dark,
cold to that Lustrous Head that lights
or strikes souls dark, with Paradise.

Man, the wild bee of time, will try
to sip the world and blind an eye
and say there seems no call to die. . . .

And so God makes the body sleep
to save the soul for modesty,
rehearsing man with nightly death
to bear the frightful stop of breath.
And so God takes my soul away
and makes my world end every day;
And I, there, with shuttered eye,
a mere breathing body lie,
all-but returned to lightless womb,
all-but inhabitant of tomb;
while God upholds me in His hand,
and if He fasten fingers hard
O I am lost or lapped in bliss
for all endless centuries!

While now I lay me down to sleep
I pray to God my soul to keep:
never to let my body die
till Christ's Body in me lie,
till Christ's Blood behind the oil
leaving anointing hand assoil
lid, and limb, and lip, and ear,
and nostril, till the spirit's clear.
Ah then I'll lay me down to sleep
and Father, Son and Spirit keep
my soul until my body leap.
Until my body leap from clay
on all mankind's Uprising Day,
and down-sent soul and body sprung
shall rise together, rung by rung,
and I that was with worm and clod
in my own flesh shall see my God.

JOHN GALLEN

LINES ON THE DEATH OF A CAT

It is so important that my grief be not absurd.
Some part of me is under earth with the cat:
The black-and-white, the woman-looking cat—
(Children sob for dogs, dead aunts only frighten
them)
This is the stammering sincerity of the humbled.

It is so important that you should not laugh—
Some life that loved me is sordidly ceased.
Me out of a world of betters this free warm thing
Sought me and me at every instant. Who now
Seeks so? None. I pray you do not smile:
For o it is so important my grief be not absurd.

ROBERT GRAVES

THE HAUNTED HOUSE

'Come, surly fellow, come! A song!'
  What, fools? sing to you?
Choose from the clouded tales of wrong
  And terror I bring to you:

Of a night so torn with cries,
  Honest men sleeping
Start awake with rabid eyes,
  Bone-chilled, flesh creeping,

Of spirits in the web-hung room
  Up above the stable,
Groans, knockings in the gloom,
  The dancing table,

Of demons in the dry well
  That cheep and mutter,
Clanging of an unseen bell,
  Blood choking the gutter,

Of lust filthy past belief
  Lurking unforgotten,
Unrestrainable endless grief
  In breasts long rotten.

A song? What laughter or what song
  Can this house remember?
Do flowers and butterflies belong
  To a blind December?

ROBERT GREACEN

THE BIRD

I

A bird flew tangent-wise to the open window.
His face was a black face of black, unknowing death;
His eyes threw the grim glint of sharpened stones,
That children pile by unfrequented roads.

And that night, dreaming into a rapture of cardboard
  life,
I started at the lean face of the bird:
A crow I think it was; but it was also death:
And sure enough there was the crisp telegram next
  morning.

I placed my mirror to the flat, unfiltered light,
But the razor cut me, in spite of the guarantee;
And I knew it was not the razor, but the ebony beak,
That slashed the base of my left nostril.

II

I loved the man who lay in the cheap coffin.
It was he first showed me the damp, stereoscopic fields
Of County Down; and now he was away to farm
The curving acres of his jealous God.

I loved the ploughing of his sun-caught brow,
And the hay-lines and chicken-feathers in his hair,
That was hay itself; the strongly cobbled boots,
And the swaying, coloured idiom of his mind.

And now he was lying with the Holy Bible under his
  chin,
Sorry only to have died before harvest and turf-cutting:
Lying dead in the room of rafters and the grey, stopped
  clock—
Because of the hatred of the bird I did not kill.

III

Sometimes now, years after, I am nakedly afraid in mid-
  winter,
And ashamed to be afraid of an incessant beak,
That raps a symphony of death on the window-panes,
Of the window I dare not throw wide open.

But one evening, just before I go to bed to die,
There will be the black face of black, unknowing death,
Flying past my open window; there will be the black
  bird,
With poison in his beak, and hatred in his wings.

ONE RECENT EVENING

One recent evening, when time and space were standing
  still,
He crossed the road flanked by air-raid rubble,
And came to a bridge where water stood below.
The sky was flushed with red and very spacious.

The soldiers paced—one of them with bayonet fixed—
Around the firm, broad-breasted, sand-bag fort.
(His brother had defiled the earth.)
The sound of trumpets slashed the dim horizon lines.

And then he felt War's impact for individuals—
How it sent one to signal across seas from an oil-tanker,
Another with wound and suitcases from a line of lean
houses. . . .
Tongues of air or sea, of land or fear, divide and
conquer us.

Walking beside the river, he forgot the shells that poise
In the city of his alternate love and hate:
He forgot the obscenities of roof and window,
The mad catharsis of the thoroughfares.

Men must not weep, he thought, or show a too-great love
For those who sleep under debris or beside ditches. . . .
'It is feared the death-roll will be heavy.'
Collective anguish has no eyes to wipe.

And he, being then an observer, dazed by lack of sleep,
Was conscious only of his unwilling senses,
Of his refusal to accept man's malice or his stupidity . . .
While the soldiers paced—one of them with bayonet
fixed.

A SERVANT GIRL'S LETTER TO HER FAITHLESS LOVER

To you, holding in spent hands all seasons' memories,
Bush and briar, thorn and thistle and tree,
I send my love all wrapped and sealed
With the tense, white paper of my sentiment.
Crying in the various nights of muffled rain
(O live lead lash on the window sill)
For you are frozen and alien from my side,
I send my freshness and my ardour

To you, folding on hard palms all seasons' memories,
Gorse and foxglove, berry and subtle, humming bee,
I post my love all crumpled and sealed
With the gum of lips you stealing stormed to starve.

SPEECH BEFORE WINTER

It comes again. The spin to the year's end
Circles to its last full stop. I defend
The fires of autumn that purr on the ground,
The stacked-up leaves, the twitching gusts that
sound,
The drawn silences here in this island,
Where the slant and pace of life are still bland.
The autumn swerves with equable pulse,
But summer eyes have turned from joy long since.
O what's the use of limping sentiment,
That crinkles the shell of my still content,
Who am more free when the great winds are loose,
More free when frames of mind restrict my choice?
Wandering winterward as vagrant leaf,
Without the saving grace of hope or grief,
All my aloneness blossoms into pain,
Plots on my pattern's rim another stain.
Come, let me end this chapter: let me close
The dog-eared chronicle that spites repose!
Exile from love's the only bitterness,
That gives this unmanned heart its trembling
guess.
O what's the use of limping sentiment,
That wrinkles the shell of my smooth content.

POEM TO K.D.

I send you greetings, Kay, now in this exiled time
From this careless Augustan city of grace and slums.
Where in Merrion Square the whispers of death
Gauze over the rhododendrons and the parched grass.
I greet you from a neutral country in a neutral hour
When the blood pace slows and nothing stirs
But the leaves in the parks, so gently;
So gently that not even the newspaper headlines
Can fluster the plumes of swans, gliding, gliding,
As on a lake of fire, fringed by pink water.
The pulse of life is faint, as in a trance,
As we await the backwash of hate's last outrage.
All Europe's continent pivots, for me, in Stephen's
Green:
Your Warsaw and Normandy fester in happy Hampstead,
Cupped in a shell of gentleness, withdrawn from the
terror
That, fevered with swift desire, strides beyond our
barricades. . . .
But everywhere, we see the uncharted darkness melt,
We see the sun pour on the sap-drained faces,
The oil of joy press motion in the wheels of love
The masks fall off, the undying day return!

SAM HARRISON

POEM

All day, resplendent in the sunny weather,
their slender smokestacks feathered and serene
as ladies walking on Edwardian lawns,
the paddle-steamers cross the summer water—
slowly they travel to the aching distance,
each with a trailing wake of waves that roll
a fugitive white ribbon down the shore.

All night my thoughts, strung out in coloured lights,
follow their gentle journeys and a fire
is burning on the mountain. . . . Though its ashes
are long since scattered, while the life that netted
the lake with flowing patterns has departed,
I still return, a lonely ghost, to watch
the ships of yesterday go softly by.

POEM FOR IONA

Through the black balcony whose metal petals
cluster in twisted patterns at my window,
I view the street, smooth river under brief
veneer of rain, light-smeared and flowing south,
fleeing the stony canyons of the town.

But soon a memory disturbs the scene—
the iron flowers tremble into life
and there, beyond them, lies our summer lake
where ripple-shadows rake the shaking reeds
and the embrace of water brings release.

Then, for a moment, the dividing power
of time and space diminishes until
I feel that you are near me once again,
and hear you call across the fluid world
as though July had never passed away.

THE HOUSE REBORN

Within this house, all summer, there has been
the vacant desolation that belongs
to things the tide of life has left behind—
the mute familiar agony that clings
to tattered ranks of disembodied clothes
ancestral in museums, or empty chairs
standing in last-night attitudes. But now,
no longer derelict, she knows again
the flow of life through corridor and room:
while autumn trees strip down to twig and branch,
reminders of the soul-forsaken bone,
she celebrates her own defiant spring
and her unshuttered windows, gay with light,
mock the defeated landscape they survey.

POEM IN JUNE

Eternity encountered on the stair
chains and enchants me—standing there, I see
the tide of green, that, crowned with foaming
  blossom,
leaps all around the house, come seeping through
each crack and crevice in the walls, until,
drowned in a scented silence, world is one,
undying, indivisible, complete.

O moment of strange certainty, if I
could only compass you and hold you fast,
I'd cling to you as close as any lover;
but time compels and I must leave you, climb
to my uneasy room set high above
the sombre city that will never cease
its lost unhappy crying in the night.

THE DANCERS

This is the Grand Pavilion
where once the wanton music played,
hearty and heartless, for the sprightly dancers
under the dangling chandeliers' long icicles
in that lost era of parade,
complacency and bicycles,
which flourished twenty years, or so, before
my days began. Here's where they took the floor
for polka, waltz-cotillion,
schottische, veleta, lancers.

Time, who can deftly alter
summer to winter, noon to night,
with practised sleight of hand has cracked and
crumbled
mirror and cornice, put his finishing touches
on every reveller—made white
the blackest of moustaches
and brought to grief each padded pompadour.
High-stepping filly, dashing paramour,
caught in the selfsame halter,
by him, at last, are humbled.

And yet the great magician
has failed somehow, for all his pains,
tricks of the trade and hocus-pocus fingers,

to fool completely—in this faded splendour
a subtler charm than his remains,
compels us to surrender
our feelings to the past, almost as though
the dancers here, one night, were set aglow
by some supreme emotion
so strong that it still lingers.

SPRING PROSPECT

The trees, whose dismal skeletons conspired
in sinister imbroglio on the hills
all winter through, at last discard
their dark designs and frivolously toss
the newest frills
of blossom like the dancers in a chorus,
with such seductive froufrou that we pose
no limit to the luck that lies before us.

Surely we shall be summer's darlings too,
glad when she leads us gently by the hands
on idle journeys down the blue
enchanted vistas the horizon hides
to distant lands
as opulent as El Dorado—places
where sunlight, green and gold beneath closed lids
will fête us with extravagant caresses.

Hopeful again, though cheated in the past
by days whose lavish promise proved to be
too lightly given, we forecast
a future that will flourish like a rose,
for how can we
do otherwise when spring, superb commando,
captures our hearts and on his bugle blows
the opening phrases of the year's crescendo?

GEORGE HETHERINGTON

FEATHERS

'The wings of life are plumed with the feathers of death.'
—RALEIGH

I

This is the final death, Death's death indeed,
The spreading stain of life due measure meeting,
A sighing wind silenced in that hollow reed.

A formal bow, a smile, some mode of greeting—
Being among friends, pray pardon the delay—
We had some work to do, were drinking, eating,

Sleeping or waking, we forgot the day;
So the hour took us unawares, surprising
Some trivial task or unimportant play;

The moment's idleness some dream devising
To clothe its awful nakedness and fill
The void between the sun's rest and its rising.

This is the final death: but not until
This moment had we thought on death; a slumber
Took us, we said, or we imagined still

Waters, the ancient boatman, memory's lumber
Dragged out to furnish that unfurnished room,
A thought without a picture, name or number;

Thought of Elija climbing the heavens, doom
Opening cavernous doors or that old bitch
Fumbling to snap the life-thread on the loom;

Thought of a wheel broken, a dropped stitch
An interrupted song, arrested gesture,
The whiteclad operator on the switch,

The surgeon's knife, new life, a change of vesture.

II

Dying in October, the last leaves falling,
Her death was a spring morning, an Easter offering,
So lightly she relinquished life and climbed
That ancient stairway, rickety with time,
Imagination's skyward passageway.

Chrysanthemums in flower, the dahlia's blazing
Image of a sun now fading, cooling,
Remind us of the falling year, the falling
Sap, life ebbing; so, in October, we,
Walking in a golden sunset, came
Suddenly on some ruinous old tower,
Its turrets broken, age climbing the walls
With the false green of ivy leaves, the lying
Pretence of sap and strength and underneath
The clawing tendrils eating in the stone.
Grass paved the threshold and that truer green
Glimmered upon the inner walls, the fallen
Stair, the arch; we, if we entered, entered
Not space but time and, if we breathed, we breathed
Not air but some green essence of the past,
Moved in a sea and knew the sea's disease.

So, in this ageing tower of the mind,
The crumbling mortar sifts between the stones,
Moss covers every creeping rift and soon
The falling roof lets in the calm, the cool
Unchanging tide of stars its arch exiled
So many years ago.

III

This house now empty is, by every door
The threescore ten-year tenantry have fled;
Seeing the rooftree tottering, the floor
Sagging beneath the feet, each shook his head
And sighed and made his last adieus and went.
But if this be the final death, whereby
Death also dies and every discontent,
Wherefore be discontented, wherefore sigh?

Indeed, this is not death at all, for death
Is every day's event, an hourly thing,
The feathers plumed along the living wing,
Pledged in the age-old bargaining for breath—
Albeit peaceful, proud or violent,
The hour's reward, the day's emolument.

JOHN HEWITT

IRELAND

We Irish pride ourselves as patriots
and tell the beadroll of the valiant ones
since Clontarf's sunset saw the Norsemen
broken....
Aye, and before that too we had our heroes:
but they were mighty fighters and victorious.
The later men got nothing save defeat,
hard transatlantic sidewalks or the scaffold....

We Irish vainer than tense Lucifer
are yet content with half a dozen turf,
and cry our adoration for a bog,
rejoicing in the rain that never ceases,
and happy to stride over sterile acres,
or stony hills that scarcely feed a sheep.
But we are fools, I say, ignorant fools
to waste the spirit's warmth in this cold air,
to spend our wit and love and poetry
on half a dozen turf and a black bog.

We are not native here or anywhere.
We were the keltic wave that broke over Europe,
and ran up this bleak beach among these stones:
but when the tide ebbed were left stranded here
in crevices, and ledge-protected pools
that have grown salter with the drying up
of the great common flow that kept us sweet
with fresh cold draughts from deep down in the
ocean.

So we are bitter, and are drying out
in terrible sourness in this lonely place:
and what we think is love for usual rock,
or old affection for our customary ledge,
is but forgotten longing for the sea
that cries far out and calls us to partake
in his great tidal movements round the earth.

POEM

Consider Wordsworth in his withered age
his high song over in ten eager years,
the chill words spilled upon the barren page
that offer boredom's armistice from tears:
yet the old hand set long in habit now,
must rime and stanza every trivial dawn
must lift the silver locks and press the brow
contemplative although the gleam is gone.

Admit the pity, bidding others rise
with face and gesture flushed with burning youth
and pass their images before your eyes
interrogating each for utter truth—
the seaborne Shelley, and the coughing lad,
the ranting gauger, and the limping lord,
and Owen whispering to the deaf and mad
with blood-smeared lip his pitiable word.

These by the leaping levels of their blood
could pour no more into the glutted horn,
for they had travelled every altitude
potential in the stars when they were born.
The end of each lay coiled within the glass.
Whose fault the crystal held a central flaw?

Through what more convolutions could they pass?
Who heard the watcher mumble what he saw?

What then of those who had the will to end
the reiveless complications of the cord—
the poisoned Chatterton without a friend,
the drugsick poet leaping overboard?
The death within those wills but planted firm
the maggot in the music: you shall see
the lovely architecture of the worm
in coral cast of white sterility.

This way or this: to take what fate may grant;
a singing summer and a barren fall
and empty winter nights when ignorant
the heart owls round its own memorial;
or the pale face that winces at defeat
and will not brace the logic of despair:
or gay among the masks that throng the street
the merry eyes of one who does not care
because he knows by heart his span and reach
and estimates the chances time may give.
The crafty seaman by the bloody ditch
heard deadmen's drivel and preferred to live.

THE GLENS

Groined by deep glens and walled along the west
by the bare hilltops and the tufted moors,
this rim of arable that ends in foam
has but to drop a leaf or snap a branch
and my hand twitches with the leaping verse
as hazel twig will wrench the straining wrists
for untapped jet that thrusts beneath the sod.

Not these my people, of a vainer faith
and a more violent lineage. My dead
lie in the steepled hillock of Kilmore
in a fat country rich with bloom and fruit.
My days, the busy days I owe the world,
are bound to paved unerring roads and rooms
heavy with talk of politics and art.
I cannot spare more than a common phrase
of crops and weather when I pace these lanes
and pause at hedge gap spying on their skill
so many fences stretch between our minds.

I fear their creed as we have always feared
the lifted hand between the mind and truth.
I know their savage history of wrong
and would at moments lend an eager voice,
if voice avail, to set that tally straight.

And yet no other corner in this land
offers in shape or colour all I need
for sight to torch the mind with living light.

THE LITTLE LOUGH

There in a bare place, in among the rocks,
grey rounded boulders shoulder'd from the ground,
where no field's big enough to yield three stacks
and corn grows on a fistful of black land,
is a small narrow lake, narrow and brown,
with whistling rushes elbow'd here and there.
And in the middle is a grassy stone
that heron or some other wanderer
will stilt on darkly.

Sometimes there will rise
a squawking mallard with a startling spray,
heading far inland, that the swift eyes lose
in the low mist that closes round the day.

Though many things I love should disappear
in the black night ahead of us, I know
I shall remember, silent crouching there,
your pale face gazing where the stiff rods grow,
seeking between the tall stems for the last
black chick the grebe is cruising round to find,
my pointing finger showing it not lost
but shelter'd only from the ruffling wind.

TOWNLAND OF PEACE

Once walking in the country of my kindred
up the steep road to where the tower-topped mound
still hoards their bones, that showery August day
I walked clean out of Europe into peace:
for every man I met was relevant,
gathering fruit or shouting to his horse,
sawing his timber, measuring his well.
The little appletrees with crooked arms
that almost touched the bright grass with the weight
of their clenched fruit, the dappled calves that
browsed
under the melting sunlight of the orchard,
the white hens slouching round the rusty trough
the neat-leafed damsons with the smoky beads
the rain had failed to polish, and the farms
back from the road but loud with dog and can
and voices moving, spelt no shape of change,
belonging to a world and to an age

that has forgotten all its violence,
save when a spade rasps on a rusty scabbard.

Old John, my father's father, ran these roads
a hundred years ago, before the Famine,
up the steep brae to school or through the gap
to the far house with milk, or dragging slow
to see his mother buried at Kilmore.
I ponder, walking steadily, my aim
to stretch my lags beside a parson's fire
in the next parish. As the road goes by
with house and hedge and tree and stook-lined field
and apples heavy on the crouching boughs
I move beside him. Change is far away,
where a daft world gone shabby makes its war
among the crumbled streets or in the plains
that show black fire-crisped rafters and smashed
  hearths
from Poland to the Yiang-tse, where the people,
slow-phrased, are whipped and beaten into thought
that well may shoulder continents for power
and new societies of steel and truth;
but here's the age they've lost.

The boys I met
munching their windfalls, coming late from school
are like that boy a hundred years ago;
the same bare kibes, the same drab heirloom rags,
but they must take another road in time.
His fortune summoned him across the sea
to the brave heyday of the smoking mills.
The bearded man who jolted in his cart,
giving his friendly answer to my word
uncertain if my track were right or left,
might have been he, if luck had left him here

or time had checked its ticking. Had I passed
a woman by a gate I should have paused
to crack about the year the Lough was frozen
and merry crowds devoured the roasted ox
beneath the bright stars of that coldest winter,
to ask if she had lost her mother too
from fever that the Famine bred, or if
she bore my family name. There's every chance
she would have, for the name is common there
as berries in the hedges anywhere.

PEARSE HUTCHINSON

WATER

The sword of the sun is white on the water;
fire sparks out of it, sprays the poplar-green.
This marine and somber splendor makes tawdry
Wisping mauve clouds.

This flaring loveliness of the fluent sea
reminds me of others akin, different:
young, lisping laughter of a mountain stream,
Flipping the furze;

The falling over cataracts; the filling
a valley; the falling from aspergilia
of angels in astral cathedrals; the spilling
And ranting of rain;

On a red roof, the furious fingers of Mór
are tomtoms ten times quickened; soft-singing
harps for Lir's minstrelsy to pluck are the plashes
On amber-waved shore;

Look, in the park, the fountain is dancing!
Ribbons of lace and froth, and foam-bandanas
are the raiment—like a sleek seal at the circus
It balances a ball;

Sharply the white efflorescence of ocean
bashes and busses the rocks. Crossing to the island
the boisterous water makes brief, gleaming, glass
bangles,
As I feather my oar.

THE RIVER

The white swans and the single celestial black
manœuvred with dignity out of our way as we glided
over the pond in the park
and the less dexterous humans, with whom we
  collided,
laughed and shouted and smiled.

I sat at the rudder in my Sunday ensemble;
my uncle rowed and grunted at the long, splashing
  oars,
that shot up jets of water, jets of jewelled water,
to fasten as beads on his ginger mustachios,
and he longed for the voyage to be over.

Two aunts perched upright, idle, talkative, witty;
they fingered their spinster-finery, now and again. . . .
I relished an ice-cream cone, and thought of the river;
the great broad river of ships, that seared like a topaz
  flame
the land of mountain and plain.

VALENTIN IREMONGER

HECTOR

Talking to her, he knew it was the end,
The last time he'd speed her into sleep with kisses:
Achilles had it in for him and was fighting mad.
The roads of his longing she again wandered,
A girl desirable as midsummer's day.

He was a marked man and he knew it,
Being no match for Achilles whom the gods were
backing.
Sadly he spoke to her for hours, his heart
Snapping like sticks, she on his shoulder crying.
Yet, sorry only that the meaning eluded him,

He slept well all night, having caressed
Andromache like a flower, though in a dream he
saw
A body lying on the sands, huddled and bleeding,
Near the feet a sword in bits and by the head
An upturned, dented helmet.

POEM IN THE DEPTHS OF SUMMER

(for Sheila)

Here now, again in this garden, I watch the summer
Burn away, June alight,
The season's torch crackling: and O among the flowers,
My childhood drumming
On my memory, nights

And days of red-faced vigour I remember when the
  hours,
Each one of them a long lane, faced me and, brave
        Child I, I essayed them unafraid.

Gripped in my fist the burning season then each hour's
        Holes and corners lit
Up brightly and slyly I hid myself chuckling with joy;
        And the roistering flowers,
        Through the slits
Of their lives, hopped out and searched for me, a boy
Free as air evading them, shouting and laughing and
  running
        Round each day's turning.

Lost long since those days: but, girl, you, who came
        To me with the good
Weather this year, the lamb and the crocus, the birds,
        Have suddenly made
        Them again real. Could
Summer have presented me flowers topping you with
  your words
Of joy, laughing among the hours, calling to me gaily
        Love is never-failing?

Summer flickers down, I know, but, my darling, we
        Have something on tap
To tide us from year to year: a reserve of love,
        Deep and free;
        And, though winter, perhaps,
Invest us, here we have sustenance, over and above
Our possible needs—till like trees we blossom
        Again, our lives' leaves tossing.

LACKENDARRAGH

And it was summer the day—late as usual, the middle
Of August, I think, and I thought how then little
    If any should die on a red evening
And hollow-chested Maulin and big-dugged Old Boleys
  pinned up
    That Sunday right then for me
      Wishing me more luck
Any day. O it was sweet in the valleys gleaming
    With girls to go taunting
And thwarting the evening that night and the next
  season
  All over the shoulder of Boleys warily peering.

And lucky was I, knew I it, to cradle my hands round
A sunray at six, in my twenty-first year on the ground,
    The days going down like armies;
But the river was talking fast, you were laughing, I
  couldn't be bothered
    Thinking how later I'd like to remember
      Odd sunrays like gossip.
Had later been mentioned I'd only have said 'What
  harm is
    It laughing like this, though September
Be down round the corner?' We were young, we were
  gay
And rich in the worship of a simple day.

O younger than summer easily, the apple-hung and the
  berry-studded
Days dropping ripe into our hands, walking the wooded
    Inclines of the valleys, we had nothing
  To do with death, although around us already, being
  August, the candles
    Of autumn flared out one by one

And summer her bangles,
Her jewels, her castanets and daring dresses was putting
Away sorrowfully: all being done
With; we were the last romantics there and then, flaunting
Our hearts asleeve, by the log-bridged river ranting.

Still on the air, though than I older far, the river
Unscripted larks, dayfree now as then, never
The poor mouth on or a grumble;
But down in the valley this later August grieves,
I see, the green exotic summer,
A revelry of leaves
Frittering out ineptly; and I, hearing the black tick in the year, wonder
When was our tuppenny-coloured
World: the river talks fast but I can't answer,
Knowing now each minute the last one cancels

—Knowing Time, that brings the leaf to book but leaves
A river gabble away a good Sunday any year,
For winter, the old wound, probes
In the heel of this season. Bleakly the bluff I essay,
Hoping defeat has its pride
Whatever it may
Be: for love will be missing in the latter end, an old
Shoe worn out and cast by,
Left rotting on some forgotten road, long before and far away
Over the hills on a perhaps like this religious day.

ICARUS

As, even to-day, the airman, feeling the plane sweat
Suddenly, seeing the horizon tilt up gravely, the wings shiver,

Knows that, for once, Daedalus has slipped up badly,
Drunk on the job, perhaps, more likely dreaming, high-flier Icarus,
Head butting down, skidding along the light-shafts
Back, over the tones of the sea-waves and the slipstream, heard
The gravel-voiced, stuttering trumpets of his heart.

Sennet among the crumbling courtyards of his brain the mistake
Of trusting somebody else on an important affair like this;
And, while the flat sea approaching buckled into oh! avenues
Of acclamation, he saw the wrong story fan out into history,
Truth, undefined, lost in his own neglect. On the hills,
The summer-shackled hills, the sun spanged all day;
Love and the world were young and there was no ending:

But star-chaser, big-time-going, chancer Icarus
Like a dog on the sea lay and the girls forgot him
And Daedalus, too busy hammering another job,
Remembered him only in pubs. No bugler at all
Sobbed taps for the young fool then, reported missing,
Presumed drowned, wing-bones and feathers on the tides
Drifting in casually, one by one.

POEM

Elizabeth, frigidly stretched,
On a spring day surprised us
With her starched dignity and the quietness
Of her hands clasping a black cross.

With book and candle and holy-water dish
She received us in the room with the blind down.
Her eyes were peculiarly closed and we knelt
shyly,
Noticing the blot of her hair on the white pillow.

We met that evening by the crumbling wall
In the field behind the house where I lived
And talked it over but could find no reason
Why she had left us whom she had liked so much.

Death, yes, we understood: something to do
With age and decay, decrepit bodies.
But here was this beautiful one aloof and prim,
Who would not answer our furtive whispers.

Next morning, hearing the priest call her name,
I fled outside being full of certainty
And cried my seven years against the church's
stone wall.
For eighteen years I did not speak her name

Until this autumn day when, in a gale,
A sapling fell outside my window, its branches
Rebelliously blotting the lawn's green. Suddenly,
I thought
Of Elizabeth, frigidly stretched.

SEÁN JENNETT

THE ISLAND

This island is the world's end. Beyond
the wide Atlantic drives its thunderous tides
backwards and forwards, beating on the land
time out of mind, a hammer on the heart,
and the storms of the west race from the huge
infinity of sea, gathering anger,
and split their bellies and their fists of rage
against the island's shattered, silent mountain.

The puffins and the rabbits own the land
and the gull and the circling ravenous eagle
and the seals bark on the edge of the sound
between the black rocks where the sea beats.
Where man trod once and wore the hard earth
 bare
the green illimitable grass
creeps back, over the garden and the gear
that fished the sea and farmed the ungenerous soil.

A lizard by a loosened door
peers into an abandoned room,
twisting his nostrils to the mummied air
that bore the shape of words, a cradle tale,
or some young girl's fresh, careless, idle song:
the sea wind and the subtle rain
break down all things at last, even the strong
stone of the wall, and the stubborn heart.

And yet they loved this island. Its hard rock
became their bone, its meagre earth their flesh,
the sea their tide of blood; and in the black
night they turned its sullenness to song.
The dancing foot that stirred the scattered sand
is quiet now or heavy overseas
and the singing voice has only songs that wound
with bitterness. The land is dead.

THE WIND

The tall wind rose and rushed across the land
shouting, shaking with his careless limbs
even the large oak and the lithe long elm
even the living fortress of the heart.

Under the scud of sky the dry bones sang
out of the lush grave and the lonely wood:
the wind shattered their bright column of words
and flung its jewels in the living hand.

A bone sang how even the living bear
the cloth of flesh for temporary grace,
sang how the smiling or the angry face
is listed in the catalogue of death.

A rib sang how the thoughtless spring had grown
to idle, heavy summer; and how summer passed
in tears to autumn; how at last
the tooth of winter bared the grieving bone.

A skull sang how beyond the coil of flesh,
beyond anxiety and the grief of blood,
beyond the bickering and the anger, cool
lands lie, peace ineluctable, and rest.

These words the wild derisive wind let fall
and drove them down with anger; and the ear
half understood and held them in its care
against the warrior and against the fool.

MY SUBTLE AND PROCLAMANT SONG

Our tears have fallen for this world of stone:
these wrinkled rocks have wept, yes even these
that bubbled out under a glaring sun
for these cold islands in the desolate seas.

Time lifted to the gape of a dead moon
draws in his lines among the water weeds
and weeps for us: the weak and rebel man
who cries defiance in the child he breeds,

and, breathing smoke along the level air
of winter, works out his sin of pride
without repentance, that no god shall dare
to drive his anger through the dusty shroud.

Yet in this unborn infant shall I live
through following time, who bend the knee to
death,
And flattering nothing that, even in love,
this carious bone shall be my monolith.

For this soft child shall in my rotting years
through his wild reins adventure for new worlds,
command what has escaped me in the weirs
of inviolable time, the treasures of shells.

His flesh shall be my stone, the word he speaks
with no matter how uncaring tongue
my epitaph; his living hours and weeks
my subtle and proclamant song.

SPRING TIDE

Spring strikes and rings the root to song
and ravels out the tangled leaf in revels
of live green along the girdering iron branch,
and swings with sway of wind in grass the meadow
levels.

O now the blackbird and the thrush all day
sing sunk in hollow green, my sally tree,
and the first grasshopper chirrs in a fist of grass,
filing his fiddle sweetly at the first tuning try.

Rings on my rocking heart this rush of green
and flush of song; and flashes in the streel
of blood the new-firing sun, that all the winter,
the ember of last year, lazed through its idle
stroll;

but now flares forth with fine arousing eye
and light lancet lunges through snoring barren
sleep
and the cold care of winter cracks: the core
of careful heart upsets, and lets its wildness slip.

O now how gapes the gap of singularity.
Reins wring the rathe frame, the eager passions
goad,
augur of love; and the blaze and the burst of it
rage in the common race and coupling of blood.

THE LETTER

She has a letter, and the crinkled sheet
Stands in her hands, facing its careless scrawl
to her face, and through her morning eyes
links with the eager question on the scroll
of brain: the words have power to move, to laugh
or weep, what though the wielder lacked in skill.

On nightmare seas the letter swung, yet came
to this small village and to her own door
to-day, swung on sea and flung in air
to her; and nerveless hands and aching bodies
dare
the splitting world for this, the personal noun,
the I that means the living is her dear.

So though the danger of a world at war
lies over all, the coupling ego joins
still, and life springs from the ultimate fusion;
growing to future among the traps and gins
of a scarecrow world: but growing from barren-
ness
through shooting blades to harvest in other Junes.

MAHONEY

Then Mahoney, standing in the surf,
the convoy hanging in the misty sea
and landing forces moving up the beach,
dropped down his arms, and said
I wait, O God, I wait,
and these were his last words of common speech.

Christ in the shallows of the water walked
or in the sweaty hollow of his palm
appeared and spoke to his reluctant bone
or moved about the chambers of his skull,
the scourger of the temple, with a whip,
and in his heart also the lash had been.

So Mahoney stood and let his rifle fall
into the sea, where lug-worms claimed it, and
the servant tide; and heard his captain shout,
but did not move; and felt the weight of wheels
and tracks across the cortex of his brain;
but did not certainly hear that single shot.

Wife, children, parents, weep for him, who now
dead with the grey crabs and the starfish rests
where surges heap on him the slow and secret
  sand.
Yet even in the valleys of the sea
the dead can feel the libel, and Mahoney
in his stripped skull is tortured by a lie.

FREDA LAUGHTON

AFTERNOON IN A GARDEN AT VINECASH

Before these pellucid pavilions
Hovers the expected nuptial bee,
Hesitant at the somnolent portals,
Vermilion and crimson,
Of poppies' petulant petals.

Scaling the skyscraper of the tiered phlomis
The ant's sweet cow, the aphis, slowly
Arrives at the whorl at the fifth story,
Confronts a solemn community
Of cowled monks, yellow, regardant.

See the butterfly unscrolling the curl
Of her coiled tongue, into coronets
Spraying an anthered anthem of spilled
  spice,
A muted fanfare from maroon
Bassoons of Dutch honeysuckle.

Mouths of calceolarias mumble
Futilely the lacquered ladybird:
She presses her escape to burrow
Strawberry-ice rose and turquoise
Chicory, Siamese cat-eyed.

The near-invisible spider stilting
An eightsome reel, delicately, alone,
Races from the slow dynamic dewdrop
Tilting from lupin leaf revolving
Sunwards with expanding afternoon.

Of some compelling darkness I have drunk
By chance or some obscure deliberation.
No fulgent glory of Venetian glass
Tinctured with cinnabar this black libation.
A cup of sculptured stone embraced the draught
Perfumed with poison-ivy's maceration.

On some far island grew the great-leaved tree.
Dark as the dilated pupil of an eye
Its fruit, thick clustered on the drooping bough,
Sombre as thunder in a fermenting sky.
Some shadowy bird forsaking carrion flesh
For this more carrion fruit, imbibed its dye,

Regurgitated juices from its maw,
Distilling to a devilish subtlety
The swarthy fruit, its dusky carrion heart,
To chill the soul in helpless apathy.
In this dark draught I drank a demon in.
I pray, perform an exorcism on me.

WHERE AUTUMN POISES

Pause here awhile
Where autumn poises
On tawny foot
Before the long descent
Into the plain of winter.

Here the fruit swells
With joy along the branches;
The orchards blow
On scented horns of ripeness;
And the long grass

Strains upward,
Caresses curtseying apples.
Parting as they fall
Into deep jealous nests
In green recesses.

Walk with me here
Under laden branches,
Our faces brushing
The cheeks of apples,
Our fingers twisting

The dark lamps of plums
From their hanging places
We will paint our lips
With wet blackberries
Among the last flowers,

The umbels of the tall
Angelica's flower-cities,
The final feathers of meadowsweet
And watch September spiders
Hang out their hammocks.

THE TRUMPETS OF WATER

The trumpets of water
Shout loudly with rain.
Under the waterfall
Lives a ripe Queen.

A damson negress,
She hangs from the trees,
Mantillaed like a fountain
With waterfall lace.

To the far bleating ocean
The river sheep run.
The furred rams on their billows
Roll in the sun.

From the sea comes the King
To cut purple from green,
And the trumpets of water
Are hats for the Queen.

C. DAY LEWIS

REGENCY HOUSES

In the abandoned heaven
Light shrinks like pools on sand—
One in a million days
That dying where they stand
Image our last and leave an
Adored light behind.
Autumn is soon. We gaze
At a Regency terrace, curved
Like the ritual smile, resigned
And formidable, that's carved
On the stone face of the dead.
Shallow a breath divides us
From the formal-smiling dead.
Light leaves this shore, these shells,
The windows glazed in death,
And soon on us beneath
A first leaf falls,
And then the next night hides us.

We who in younger days,
Hoping too much, tried on
The habit of perfection,
Have learnt how it betrays
Our shrinking flesh: we have seen
The praised transparent will
Living now by reflection.
The panes darken: but still
We have seen peering out
The mad, too mobile face

Under the floral hat.
Are we living—we too
Living extravagant farce
In the finery of spent passions?
Is all we do and shall do
But the glib, habitual breathing
Of clocks where time means nothing,
In a condemned mansion?

DEPARTURE IN THE DARK

Nothing so sharply reminds a man he is mortal
As leaving a place
In a winter morning's dark, the air on his face
Unkind as the touch of sweating metal:
Simple good-byes to children or friends become
A felon's numb
Farewell, and love that was a warm, a meeting
  place—
Love is the suicide's grave under the nettles.

Gloomed and clemmed as if by an imminent ice-age
Lies the dear world
Of your street-strolling, field-faring. The senses,
  curled
At the dead end of a shrinking passage,
Care not if close the inveterate hunters creep,
And memories sleep
Like mammoths in lost caves. Drear, extinct is the
  world
And has no voice for consolation or presage.

There is always something at such times of the
  passover,

When the dazed heart
Beats for it knows not what, whether you part
From home or prison, acquaintance or lover—
Something wrong with the timetable, something
  unreal
In the scrambled meal
And the bag ready packed by the door, as though
  the heart
Has gone ahead, or is staying here for ever.

No doubt for the Israelites that early morning
It was hard to be sure
If home were prison or prison home: the desire
Going forth meets the desire returning.
This land, that had cut their pride down to the bone
Was now their own
By ancient deeds of sorrow. Beyond, there was
  nothing sure
But a desert of freedom to quench their fugitive
  yearnings.

At this blind hour the heart is informed of nature's
Ruling that man
Should be nowhere a more tenacious settler than
Among wry thorns and ruins, yet nurture
A seed of discontent in his ripest ease.
There's a kind of release
And a kind of torment in every good-bye for every
  man—
And will be, even to the last of his dark departures.

ONE AND ONE

I remember, as if it were yesterday,
Watching that girl from the village lay
The fire in a room where sunlight poured,
And seeing, in the annexe beyond, M. play
A prelude of Bach on his harpsichord.

I can see his face now, heavy and numb
With resignation to the powers that come
At his touch meticulous, smooth as satin,
Firm as hammers: I can hear the air thrum
With notes like sun-motes in a twinkling
  pattern.

Her task there fetched from the girl the innate
Tingling response of glass to a note:
She fitted the moment, too, like a glove,
Who deft and submissive knelt by the grate
Bowed as if in the labour of love.

Their orbits touched not: but the pure sub-
  mission
Of each gave value and definition
To a snapshot printed in that morning's sun.
From any odd corner we may start a vision
Proving that one and one make One.

THE ALBUM

I see you, a child
In a garden sheltered for buds and playtime,
Listening as if beguiled
By a fancy beyond your years and the flowering
  maytime.
The print is faded: soon there will be

No trace of that pose enthralling,
Nor visible echo of my voice distantly calling
'Wait! Wait for me!'

Then I turn the page
To a girl who stands like a questioning iris
By the waterside, at an age
That asks every mirror to tell what the heart's desire is
The answer she finds in that oracle stream
Only time could affirm or disprove,
Yet I wish I was there to venture a warning, 'Love
Is not what you dream'.

Next you appear
As if garlands of wild felicity crowned you—
Courted, caressed, you wear
Like immortelles the lovers and friends around you.
'They will not last you, rain or shine,
They are but straws and shadows,'
I cry: 'Give not to those charming desperadoes
What was made to be mine'.

One picture is missing—
The last. It would show me a tree stripped bare
By intemperate gales, her amazing
Noonday of blossom spoilt which promised so fair.
Yet, scanning those scenes at your heyday taken,
I tremble, as one who must view
In the crystal a doom he could never deflect—yes, I too
Am fruitlessly shaken.

I close the book;
But the past slides out of its leaves to haunt me
And it seems, wherever I look,
Phantoms of irreclaimable happiness taunt me.

Then I see her, petalled in new-blown hours,
Beside me. 'All you love most there
Has blossomed again,' she murmurs, 'all that you
missed there
Has grown to be yours.'

THE INNOCENT

A forward child, a sullen boy
My living image in the pool,
The glass that made me look a fool—
He was my judgement and my joy.

The bells that chimed above the lake,
The swans asleep in evening's eye,
Bright transfers pressed on memory
From him their gloss and anguish take.

When I was desolate, he came
A wizard way to charm my toys:
But when he heard a stranger's voice
He broke the toys, I bore the shame.

I built a house of crystal tears
Amid the myrtles for my friend:
He said, no man has ever feigned
Or kept the lustre of my years.

Later, a girl and I descried
His shadow on the fern-flecked hill,
His double near our bed: and still
The more I lived, the more he died.

Now a revenant slips between
The fine-meshed minutes of the clock
To weep the time we lost and mock
All that my desperate ditties mean.

ON THE SEA WALL

ὢς γὰρ ἐς σ' ἴδω βρόχε' ὤς με φώναις
οὐδ' ἒν ἔτ εἶκει. . . .

Sappho.

As I came to the sea wall that August day,
One out of all the bathers there
Beckoned my eye, a girl at play
With the surf-flowers. Was it the dark, dark hair
Falling Egyptian-wise, or the way
Her body curved to the spray?—

I know not. Only my heart was shaking
Within me, and then it stopped; as though
You were dead and your shape had returned to
 haunt me
On the very same spot where five years ago
You slipped from my arms and played in the
 breaking
Surges to tease and enchant me.

I could not call out. Had there been no more
Than those thickets of rusty wire to pen us
Apart, I'd have gone to that girl by the shore
Hoping she might be you. But between us
Lie tangled, severing, stronger far,
The barbed relics of love's old war.

HORNPIPE

Now the peak of summer's past, the sky is overcast
And the love we swore would last for an age seems
 deceit:
Paler is the guelder since the day we first beheld her
In blush beside the elder drifting sweet, drifting sweet.

Oh quickly they fade—the sunny esplanade,
Speed-boats, wooden spades and the dunes where we've
  lain:
Others will be lying amid the sea-pinks sighing
For love to be undying, and they'll sigh in vain.

It's hurrah for each night we have spent our love so
  lightly
And never dreamed there might be no more to spend
  at all.
It's good-bye to every lover who thinks he'll live in
  clover
All his life, for noon is over soon and night dews fall.

If I could keep you there with the berries in your hair
And your lacy fingers fair as the may, sweet may,
I'd have no heart to do it, for to stay love is to rue it
And the harder we pursue it, the faster it's away.

DO NOT EXPECT AGAIN A PHOENIX HOUR

Do not expect again a phoenix hour,
The triple-towered sky, the dove complaining,
Sudden the rain of gold and heart's first ease
Tranced under trees by the eldritch light of sundown

By a blazed trail our joy will be returning:
One burning hour throws light a thousand ways,
And hot blood stays into familiar gestures.
The best years wait, the body's plenitude.

Consider then, my lover, this is the end
Of the lark's ascending, the hawk's unearthly hover:
Spring season is over soon and first heatwave;
Grave-browed with cloud ponders the huge horizon.

Draw up the dew. Swell with pacific violence.
Take shape in silence. Grow as the clouds grew.
Beautiful brood the cornlands, and you are heavy;
Leafy the boughs—they also hide big fruit.

DONAGH MacDONAGH

THE HUNGRY GRASS

Crossing the stony silence high above sea
Where few birds nest, the careless foot may pass
From the bright safety of experience
Into the terror of the hungry grass.

Here in a year when poison from the air
First withered in despair the growth of spring
Some skull-faced wretch whom nettle could not
save
Crept on four bones to his last scattering,

Crept, and the shrivelled heart which drove his
thought
Towards platters brought in hospitality
Burst as the wizened eyes measured the miles
Like dizzy walls forbidding him the city.

Little the earth reclaimed from that poor body,
And yet, remembering him, the place has grown
Bewitched, and the thin grass he nourishes
Racks with his famine, sucks marrow from the
bone.

Note.—It is believed in many parts of Ireland that an overwhelming hunger and weakness felt at certain spots is caused by crossing 'féar gorta' or 'hungry grass' growing where some victim of the famine of 1847–8 died.

DUBLIN MADE ME

Dublin made me and no little town
With the country closing in on its streets
The cattle walking proudly on the pavements
The jobbers, the gombeenmen, and the cheats

Devouring the fair day between them
A public-house to half a hundred men
And the teacher, the solicitor and the bank clerk
In the hotel bar drinking for ten.

Dublin made me, not the secret poteen still
The raw and hungry hills of the West,
The lean road flung over profitless bog
Where only a snipe could nest

Where the sea takes its tithe of every boat
Bawneen and curragh have no allegiance of
mine
Nor the cute self-deceiving talkers of the South
Who look to the East for a sign.

The soft and dreary midlands with their tame
canals
Wallow between sea and sea remote from adven-
ture,
And Northward a far and fortified province
Crouches under the lash of arid censure.

I disclaim all fertile meadows, all tilled land
The evil that grows from it and the good,
But the Dublin of old statutes, this arrogant city,
Stirs proudly and secretly in my blood.

AT LARACOR

We stood about a grave at Laracor
Each cloistered in his thought, the naked wind
Savagely tearing at the tender body,
The frozen landscape dominated by the simple fact,
The glistening coffin. Fear and hope and pity
Simplified our hearts, the city and
The complex graph of living were erased
And the blind emotions fastened on damp earth.
For an hour the lines upon the face
Were meaningless, the courses that they charted
Abandoned; and looking at poet and businessman,
Painter and dramatist I saw age
Stripped from the bone and children, innocent
And lovely, standing in the bitter meadow;
Fear tore at my throat that was not fear
Of death, for in each lined and disillusioned
Face I saw childhood twisted and torn.
And as the coffin sank beneath the green
Level of our world I mourned the child
Lost in the leaden body, and all the children
Staring so bleakly from the ageing eyes.

A PARABLE

Splendidly furnished like a god the hero
Steps to the field, secure in influence
Yokes the fire-breathing bulls with brazen feet
And tooth by tooth ploughs in the seeds of strife.
Cross-bow and spear and crescent scimitar
Flower instantly, and cruder threats of war
The bully bludgeon and the eager knife
Are in a moment joined, and stare-eyed men
Who spring blood-crazy from the earth are slain.

Jason stands armed, but troop on crazy troop
The dragon-born insensates with new weapons
Are self-annihilated; musket and carbine,
Cannon and Greek Fire thicken the air,
And soon great shining weapons, beautiful
And compact with all mind's genius, devastate
Millions of seedling warriors; but Cadmus' field
Is fertile still, and millions spring to birth
Who in an instant turn again to earth.

When the last madman dies and silence comes
The hero lifts his spear and haughtily
Shouts to the gathered Greeks, 'What man will
dare
Meet me in combat now?' And fools are found
To face him on the saturated ground.

ANACH CUAN

The sorriest themes stick in a nation's ears—
A boatload of western men drowned on a strand
Or an encounter at a village fair—
But stuffed and dressed and decked out to look grand
Led to a festive air
And loaded down with colourable words:
These sluts of chance have strutted with the bards.

Our days are a bit like that and even our years—
Boastful Saturday night forgotten the next morning
And maybe some modest Monday that brought in
death
Birth, or a wedding, or confirmed a warning,
Is blown sky-high in a breath
Fills all the air with a glory of pumice and fire
Bursting rockets of emotion or spent sticks of desire.

BRÍDÍN VESEY

(after the Irish)

I would marry Brídín Vesey
Without a shoe or petticoat,
A comb, a cloak or dowry
Or even one clean shift;
And I would make novena
Or imitate the hermits
Who spend their lives in fasting
All for a Christmas gift.
O cheek like dogwood fruiting,
O cuckoo of the mountain,
I would send darkness packing
If you would rise and go
Against the ban of clergy
And the sour lips of your parents
And take me at an altar-stone
In spite of all Mayo.

That was the sullen morning
They told the cruel story,
How scorning word or token
You rose and went away.
'Twas then my hands remembered,
My ears still heard you calling,
I smelt the gorse and heather
Where you first learned to pray.
What could they know, who named you
Of jug and bed and table,
Hours slipping through our fingers,
Time banished from the room?
Or what of all the secrets
We knew among the rushes
Under the Reek when cuckoos
Brightened against the moon?

You are my first and last song,
The harp that lilts my fingers
Your lips like frozen honey,
Eyes like the mountain pool,
Shaped like the Reek your breast is,
Whiter than milk from Nephin,
And he who never saw you
Has lived and died a fool.
Oh, gone across the mearing
Dividing hope from sadness
What happy townland holds you?
In what country do you reign?
In spite of all the grinning lads
At corner and in haybarn,
I'll search all Ireland over
And bring you home again.

THE VETERANS

Strict hairshirt of circumstance wears the flesh
On delicate bones;
Years of counter and office, the warped mesh
Of social living, dropping on stones,
Wear down all that was rough and worthy
To a common denominator of dull tones.

So these, who in the sixteenth year of the century
Saw their city, a Phoenix upturned,
Settle under her ashes and bury
Hearts and brains that more frantically burned
Than the town they destroyed, have with the
corrosion of time
Spent more than they earned;

And with their youth has shrunk their singular
mystery
Which for one week set them in the pulse of their age,
Their spring adventure petrified in history,
A line on a page,
Betrayed into the hands of students who question
Oppressed and oppressor's rage.

Only the dead beneath their granite signatures
Are untroubled by the touch of day and day,
Only in them the first rich vision endures;
Those over clay
Retouch in memory, with sentiment relive,
April and May.

PATRICK MacDONOGH

SHE WALKED UNAWARE

O, she walked unaware of her own increasing beauty
That was holding men's thoughts from market or plough,
As she passed by intent on her womanly duties
And she without leisure to be wayward or proud;
Or if she had pride then it was not in her thinking
But thoughtless in her body like a flower of good breeding.
The first time I saw her spreading coloured linen
Beyond the green willow she gave me gentle greeting
With no more intention than the leaning willow tree.

Though she smiled without intention yet from that day
forward
Her beauty filled like water the four corners of my being,
And she rested in my heart like a hare in the form
That is shaped to herself. And I that would be singing
Or whistling at all times went silently then;
Till I drew her aside among straight stems of beeches
When the blackbird was sleeping, and she promised that
never
The fields would be ripe but I'd gather all sweetness,
A red moon of August would rise on our wedding.

October is spreading bright flame along stripped willows
Low fires of the dogwood burn down to grey water,—
God pity me now and all desolate sinners
Demented with beauty! I have blackened my thought
In drouths of bad longing, and all brightness goes
shrouded

Since he came with his rapture of wild words that mirrored
Her beauty and made her ungentle and proud.
To-night she will spread her brown hair on his pillow
But I shall be hearing the harsh cries of wild fowl.

SOON WITH THE LILAC FADES ANOTHER SPRING

God! but this rain-sweet greenness shakes the heart,
After untimely drought, after love's lenten fast,
Seeing the tender brightness push apart
Brown walls of winter. Now to my thoughts at last
Love I have long desired, as grass desires the rain,
Returns, returns, returns; soft as a settling bird
Turning itself in the nest, softly her name has stirred,
But oh, this new-sprung joy is all shot through with
pain.

This is the selfsame wood whose branches wept
When Deirdre danced to Naisi, these tall trees
Wound aching arms above while Grainne slept,
And the immortal changeling Heloïse,
Breaking these brilliant pools with naiad feet,
Ran to her god, suddenly desolate,
Remembering Paris and the dark house hushed with
hate,
Then the long anguish took them, and the Paraclete.

Soon with the lilac fades another spring,
And one less left to live, and all our springs must die;
In all the world there lives no lasting thing
No thing in all the world, and you and I,
Mere ghostly springs of summers long since dead,
Turn to our winter with no second spring—
I have no solace from remembering
How death's cold hands will hold that arrogant head.

The old men's bat-like voices on the walls
  Were hushed when Helen passed; and even yet
Across three thousand years that shadow falls
  Upon the face of love; for men forget
No beauty branded with the mark of Cain;
  While all the thoughtless-happy fade apace,
  Still the pale virgin in the chapel face
Bids the young eyes of spring witness eternal pain.

LOUIS MacNEICE

DUBLIN

Grey brick upon brick
Declamatory bronze
On sombre pedestals—
O'Connell, Grattan, Moore—
And the brewery tugs and the swans
On the balustraded stream
And the bare bones of a fanlight
Over a hungry door
And the air soft on the cheek
And porter running from the taps
With a head of yellow cream
And Nelson on his Pillar
Watching his world collapse.

This was never my town,
I was not born nor bred
Nor schooled here and she will not
Have me alive or dead
But yet she holds my mind
With her seedy elegance,
With her gentle veils of rain
And all her ghosts that walk
And all that hide behind
Her Regency façades—
The catcalls and the pain,
The glamour of her squalor,
The bravado of her talk.

The lights jig in the river
With a concertina movement,
And the sun comes up in the morning
Like barley-sugar on the water,

And the mist on the Wicklow hills
Is close, as close
As the peasantry were to the landlord,
As the Irish to the Anglo-Irish,
As the killer is close one moment
To the man he kills,
Or as the moment itself
Is close to the next moment.

She is not an Irish town
And she is not English,
Historic with guns and vermin
And the cold renown
Of a fragment of Church Latin,
Of an oratorical phrase.
But O the days are soft,
Soft enough to forget
The lessons better learnt,
The bullet on the wet
Streets, the crooked deal,
The steel behind the laugh,
The Four Courts burnt.

Fort of the Dane,
Garrison of the Saxon,
Augustan capital
Of a Gaelic nation,
Appropriating all
The alien brought,
You give me time for thought
And by a juggler's trick
You poise the toppling hour—
O greyness run to flower,
Grey stone, grey water,
And brick upon grey brick.

THE SUNLIGHT ON THE GARDEN

The sunlight on the garden
Hardens and grows cold,
We cannot cage the minute
Within its nets of gold,
When all is told
We cannot beg for pardon.

Our freedom as free lances
Advances towards its end;
The earth compels, upon it
Sonnets and birds descend;
And soon, my friend,
We shall have no time for dances.

The sky was good for flying
Defying the church bells
And every evil iron
Siren and what it tells:
The earth compels,
We are dying, Egypt, dying

And not expecting pardon,
Hardened in heart anew,
But glad to have sat under
Thunder and rain with you,
And grateful too
For sunlight on the garden.

THE SPRINGBOARD

He never made the dive—not while I watched.
High above London, naked in the night
Perched on a board. I peered up through the bars
Made by his fear and mine but it was more than fright
That kept him crucified among the budding stars.

Yes, it was unbelief. He knew only too well
That circumstances called for sacrifice
But, shivering there, spreadeagled above the town,
His blood began to haggle over the price
History would pay if he were to throw himself down.

If it would mend the world, that would be worth while;
But he, quite rightly, long had ceased to believe
In any Utopia or in Peace-upon-Earth;
His friends would find in his death neither ransom nor
  reprieve,
But only a grain of faith—for what it was worth.

And yet we know he knows what he must do.
There above London where the gargoyles grin
He will dive like a bomber past the broken steeple,
One man wiping out his own original sin
And, like ten million others, dying for the people.

BROTHER FIRE

When our brother Fire was having his dog's day
Jumping the London streets with millions of tin cans
Clanking at his tail, we heard some shadow say
'Give the dog a bone'—and so we gave him ours;
Night after night we watched him slaver and crunch away
The beams of human life, the tops of topless towers.

Which gluttony of his for us was Lenten fare
Who mother-naked, suckled with sparks, were chill
Though cotted in a grill of sizzling air
Striped like a convict—black, yellow and red;
Thus were we weaned to knowledge of the Will
That wills the natural world but wills us dead.

O delicate walker, babbler, dialectician Fire,
O enemy and image of ourselves,
Did we not on those mornings after the 'All Clear',
When you were looting shops in elemental joy
And singing as you swarmed up city block and spire,
Echo your thought in ours? 'Destroy! Destroy!'

MUTATIONS

If there has been no spiritual change of kind
Within our species since Cro-Magnon Man
And none is looked for now while the millennia cool,
Yet each of us has known mutations in the mind
When the world jumped and what had been a plan
Dissolved and rivers gushed from what had seemed a
pool.

For every static world that you or I impose
Upon the real one must crack at times and new
Patterns from new disorders open like a rose
And old assumptions yield to new sensation;
The Stranger in the wings is waiting for his cue,
The fuse is always laid to some annunciation.

Surprises keep us living: as when the first light
Surprised our infant eyes or as when, very small,
Clutching our parents' hands we toddled down a road
Where all was blank and windless both to touch and
sight
Had we not suddenly raised our eyes which showed
The long grass blowing wild on top of the high
wall.

For it is true, surprises break and make,
As when the baton falls and all together the hands
On the fiddle-bows are pistons, or when crouched above
His books the scholar suddenly understands
What he has thought for years—or when the inveterate
  rake
Finds for once that his lust is becoming love.

NUTS IN MAY

May come up with bird-din,
And May come up with sun-dint,
May come up with water-wheels,
    And May come up with iris.

In the sun-peppered meadow the shepherds are
  old,
Their flutes are broken and their tales are told,
And their ears are deaf when the guns unfold
The new philosophy over the wold.

May come up with pollen of death,
May come up with cordite,
May come up with a chinagraph,
    And May come up with a stopwatch.

In the high court of heaven Their tailfeathers shine
With cowspit and bullspit and spirits of wine,
They know no pity, being divine,
And They give no quarter to thine or mine.

May come up with Very lights,
May come up with duty,
May come up with a bouncing cheque,
    An acid-drop and a bandage.

Yes, angels are frigid and shepherds are dumb,
There is no holy water when the enemy come,
The trees are askew and the skies are a-hum
And you have to keep mum and go to it and die
   for your life and keep mum.

May come up with fiddle-bows,
May come up with blossom,
May come up the same again,
   The same again but different.

CONVERSATION

Ordinary people are peculiar too:
Watch the vagrant in their eyes
Who sneaks away while they are talking with you
Into some black wood behind the skull
Following un—, or other realities,
Fishing for shadows in a pool.

But sometimes the vagrant comes the other way
Out of their eyes and into yours
Having mistaken you perhaps for yesterday
Or for to-morrow night, a wood in which
He may pick up among the pine-needles and
   burrs
The lost purse, the dropped stitch.

Vagrancy however is forbidden; ordinary men
Soon come back to normal, look you straight
In the eyes as if to say 'It will not happen again',
Put up a barrage of common sense to baulk
Intimacy but by mistake interpolate
Swear-words like roses in their talk.

Among these turf stacks graze no iron horses
Such as stalk, such as champ in towns and the souls
of crowds,
Here is no mass-production of neat thoughts
No canvas shrouds for the mind nor any black
hearses:
The peasant shambles on his boots like hooves
Without thinking at all or wanting to run in
grooves.

But those who lack the peasants' conspirators,
The tawny mountain, the unregarded buttress,
Will feel the need of a fortress against ideas and
against the
Shuddering insidious shock of the theory-vendors,
The little sardine men cramped in a monster toy
Who tilt their aggregate beast against our crum-
bling Troy.

For we are obsolete who like the lesser things
Who play in corners with looking-glasses and
beads;
It is better we should go quickly, go into Asia
Or any other tunnel where the world recedes,
Or turn blind wantons like the gulls who scream
And rip the edge off any ideal or dream.

ROY McFADDEN

LETTER TO A BOY IN PRISON

I who walk in the sun,
Seize hope by eager hands,
Talk with friends, hold
Quick stolen dregs of laughter
To the quivering mouth, fold
Unhappy hands in prayer,
Nervous as moths, for you
And the tired christs everywhere.

I send the green of the trees,
The various looks of the flowers,
The rippling run of the hills
And the fields at peace with the world.
Through the final motionless walls
I send the love you have missed,
The smiles you failed to find,
The mouths you might have kissed.

I send my faith and yours,
Quiet as September skies,
Sure that the day will see
In the flesh our dream of the night·
Sure that the day will free
The limbs locked deep from the sun
And open the door of your cell,
And the prison that holds us all
Walled from the sun, in hell.

1942.

EPITHALAMIUM

So you are married, girl. It makes me sad,
Somehow, to think of that: that you, once held
Between hot hands on slow white afternoons,
Whose eyes I knew down to their blackest depths
(Stirred by the small red smile and the white laugh)
Are married now. Some man whom I have not seen
Calls up the smile and the laugh, holds in his hands
The welcoming body, sees in the darkening eyes
Sufficient future in a smug white room.
I wish you well. May you have many sons
With darkening eyes and quiet gentle hands
To build a better future for their sons.
I, wed to history, pray for your peace,
That the smile be never twisted in your mouth,
And the pond of your mind never be rippled with
sorrow:
That you may sleep your sleep as the world quakes
And never see the chasms at your feet.

1942

A CRY

If it was Samson I
Would pull this madhouse down
Loud about their ears—
But I being only I
With hands like melting snow
Must thole the fools, and crown
Joy with a cap of tears.

If it was Samson I
Would raise great shouting hands
Out to the crying dawn—

But I being only I
With slave hands quiet as dew
Bind them with white prayer bands,
And put my soul in pawn.

If it was Samson I
Would move great hills of faith
Loud with my great heart's cry—
But I being only I
Loose as wind-clutched straw
Must raise pale hands at death,
Seeing no white Christ die.

1942

IRELAND—1941

In Ireland now, at autumn, fringed by war,
We banish Europe with each bolted door
And night-slammed window; huddling into the past,
Bitter, but not so bitter as the world,
We watch the heads of flame swirl in the draught,
The demon dancers on stark innocent walls,
And turn from the child-like keen of the wind in the
wires.

And think, we who are a little apart from the world,
Think of the swinging hills and running lanes
Of sun and wind, and the girlish breasts of fields
Untamed by plough, and cannot comprehend
The mass of faces crying *Crucify*:
Though the mass resolves into the single soul
Whose pulse beats soberly across the world.

In autumn now, when leaf and hope are failing,
And days, grown old, yawn earlier than before;
In autumn now, when leaves and men are falling

Memory limps backward over the twilit year,
Looking for sun and warmth of summer fields,
Now that the year drops symbols with the leaves.

In autumn now, when leaves and blood are falling,
And field and thought are dark with seasonal shadow,
In season of harvest by sickle and bayonet,
Memory limps backward over the twilit year,
Looking for sun and warmth of summer fields
Time may restore, perhaps, after the harvest . . .

THE PATTERN

Out of these hills and fierce historic fields,
Out of this froth of trees and solemn stretches
Of solitary soil where hurrying winds
Gossip and separate: out of this sky
Holding the island cupped to the ear of God:
Out of each clenched bush and soncie river
Swaggering to sea: out of the frail
Flotsam of the shipwrecked centuries,
I speak, with all their love and loss and anger.

Every stone in every crazy wall
Stumbling across the skyline, every road
Streaming like ribbon from ballooning hills,
Each alarm of whin and sudden slash
Of water knifing brown-ribbed, opulent fields,
The panic of birds loud on the heels of the day—
Push eager, arrogant fists through all my words.

The fat good-natured fields of County Down,
And the lean menace of the Antrim plains

Dark with cloud or rusted red with rain
That drifts with each slow wind down from the
  hills:
And the strange city, patient in its hates,
Bathing hands in bloody history,
Its angry martyrs urgent and alive,
Where dogma has its store of stones to fling.
And smoke flies with the handkerchief—like
  gulls
Down through the veins and arteries of streets
To the black heart pulsing its own false time:
All these are in the pattern, and the sea,
The latent sea of history always flowing,
Casting its shipwreck and its mariners
Stark on the fleeing beaches of the mind.

1943

PATRICK MAYBIN

APRIL

Come through the quiet fields; April again
has brought the primroses and daily the air
grows warmer for sap flowing and leaf unfolding.
Soon the green blades of corn will thrust from the
bare
soil, morning be loud with bird-song,
and all things eager for the coming of spring.

There is strength here, not in the brief delight
of violet or king-cup or the sheen
of bright wing in sunlight, but in the changing
of flower to fruit, in promise of good grain,
in the slow working of water upon stone,
the quick whip of the wind, and the sting of rain.

BALLYKINLAR, MAY 1940

One standing on the empty beach
beyond the sandhills threw wide his arms
with an oratorical gesture to beseech
the blue and unresponsive hills:
let now Cuchulain or some of the old gods
descend from the mountains, with chariot wheels
scything the hordes of evil wielding again
his battle-axe for freedom before all else fails.

And yet, the Red Branch withered at the last
now only a shadow in the mind of man
the victors and the victims—they are all lost

and the shed blood forgotten. Surely it were better
in these bitter days to walk by the sea's quiet margin
or humbly where the dry grass murmurs. Not out of
 the hills
must come the conquering host, but from the deep
recesses of the heart, before the darkness falls.

COLIN MIDDLETON

BEYOND

Holding a smooth white pebble to my cheek
I know that men have died for this, this ease
of soul so moulding in a moment's grace
immensities of space and time, replacing
in the quick metal of expectant clay
the grey solicitude of studious brain
with the sharp pain of shaping. Bodily
as the rose is thrust from the resilient briar
petalled and perfect, yielding to receive,
so blooms the illumined flower of prophecy
in silence, reaching out beyond the graves
of seers and prophets.

WAYFARING

To-morrow comes and I am blessed
with second sight; my yesterday
blooms wide beside the broad highway
to greet and bid a stranger rest.
Who laid the present in my hands
and called it by a common name?
My dear, the passengers who came
in this same vessel to these lands
make no demand on moon or sun
nor fashion calendars of stone
to guide our feet 'tween tide and tide
and hide us in the mountain side.

That we of man demand a cell
wherein to dwell immaculate
from dawn to dusk—and who can tell
what mite will seal the lion's fate
and over-ride as tidal waves
the grave the altar and the font
and all the little rules we make
for breaking fast and ending want,
for tending, taking, trusting; we
who seek the tender in the small:
have we no larger claim to make
than seeing for each other's sake?

All this, and all this weariness,
this weight of hatred, trade in woe,
this roundabout of doubting—Oh
deliver us, deliver us
from living, from the livelong day,
the long way out, the wrong way in,
the din to drown a lesser din,
the sin to make the sinner pay.
Come gay, come fair, come mad with pain,
come shouting through this world again,
but most with laughter come to me,
my darling, that the whole world see
that worlds exist behind such bars
and barriers against the stars.

If I am lover to the world
the whole world over, you and I
in macrocosmic sympathy
move where the nomad knows the moon
by seed in season, by the hue
or perfume of the humid night—
and I, divining what to do,

reply in kind because my sight
is focused on the same bright star:
and all you are and all I am
no other than the still small flame
we call by some affectionate name.

If I, the whole world over, strive
to see myself and seeing be
the bright shape of your mystery,
the myth upon the morning's lips,
come gay, come fair, for I am come
to be the wonder in your eye,
a silence on a twilit sea
between the passing of two ships:
and all of me and all of you
no farther than a white bird's call
from where the stars of evening sing
the small song of our wayfaring.

EWART MILNE

LISTEN, MANGAN

This is the house with the panelled door,
The Irish house in Abbey Street;
This is the house the Dean built.

And one who knocked and sought for preferment,
Crying 'Let me come in, let me come home',
Heard down the corridors the echoes go rumbling
Down the empty corridors of the house of learning,
'Let me come home, come home, come home . . .'

This is the house with the panelled door,
The Irish house in Abbey Street;
This is the house that is falling.

Listen, Mangan! (And then no more)
One who stands to-day at the door of learning
Tells you (down the corridors the echoes go
rumbling)
It was not a woman here. Here there is not bread,
Not daily bread. Do you hear, Mangan?
Do you hear, dead man? Listen, the echoes
rumbling—
The bricks falling, crashing, falling . . .

This is the house—
Get away from the house—
This was the house of learning.

THE WATERSIDE POEM

(For B. Traven, who wrote *The Death Ship*)

SHANGHAIED aboard
We signed on later because we *must*.
In a smelly cabin among charts and paraffin
We signed on for the round trip:
Where we were bound for had been left blank.

And a hard going we had of it.
You were below then, in the stokehold, while I
Swung overside in a bosun's chair
Was repainting the ship's name on the rusty bow.
Her name was, as I remember, the steamship Earth.

O and she was the yellow-skinned one,
She was the gay mulatto,
Knees-up Sally Brown we met for our sins . . .
Rolling and straining and pitching was the least of
her,
And no way to leave her: no port in the storms

Unless she was the port, for we knew no other.
You and I: cursing the day we had ever met her—
You with knuckles bleeding, scalded too with the
steam,
Raking the back-ends, trimming the bunkers—
I, sick as a dog, taking my turn at the wheel.

She cured us of harbour lights and the girls all right.
She rolled over you with the firebar weighting your
feet
In a sea of sequins sinking, that burial evening.
You slid down through the seabirds who hardly
moved—
So tired they were after the storm—to let you pass.

And I? I was cured of dying then,
And by death not answered, I mourned you, friend,
But even as you sank among the birds in your canvas
suiting
I knew I would complete the voyage in good order
Because I had a fancy to paint her name again on
the bow.

Still I mourned: and still it was nothing.
Aye, it takes iron men for an iron ship. You had not
time
To learn to wear her armour but your watch change
rang—
And again the screw churned faster, and we raised
A sunward shore with palms, with houses and flower-
ing terraces.

Listen: I say we signed, and there's no unsigning.
And the voyage is never completed, though some
may ask
What creature says this, with the sea through his eyes
looking.
We signed and there's no unsigning. Hell, no, but
she rolls,
And she rolls us like foam from her flanks, the gay
mulatto.

SPRING SONG

Now ready Meath with barley field for sowing,
as peasant courtship for hard exultant mating,
but do not speak of these to us
whose downcast eyes avoid the flash of buds.

Tell only of our sorrow and our unresting,
of echoes that twitch our spines despite us;
as we crumble in sunlit offices and bed-sittingrooms
beasts and flowers mean nothing to us.

Tell only of our sorrow and our despair:
that many lives have lived our lives many times,
that we bring nothing new to the face of things
who lean on winds and beseech the upland air.

The upland air our hiking party breathes,
the picnic fields where one of us went missing,
one we found face down among the grasses
and tiptoed away, and left him to his weeping

Slowly . . . and retraced the opal dimming lough
flanked by rusty turbines, to the bus:
Slowly, and we laughed that love is weary, wearisome.
Beasts and flowers mean nothing to us.

'IN A VALLEY OF THIS RESTLESS MIND'

I think now of latitudes solitary, Asian, and velvet,
Even while the mechanized ants march to their jungle attack,
Moving to that complete south where birds of paradise flee
In their scarlet and gold to the mating shelter of palms.

And as if wandering beneath the giant skies of the Cross,
Dissolved in the immeasurable vault that everywhere penetrates the ocean,
I am borne onward through the undark where like snowflake silently
The white body of albatross or seaplane glides down to the swell.

Even more I am haunted by world-girdling cables
Encrusted by coral and shells, along which flash messages:
Even more I am haunted by those cables tapped by deep-sea creatures,
Girdling far down on the tideless sands, girdling and gripping.

Above this the mechanized ants march and birds of paradise flee
In their scarlet and gold to the mating shelter of palms.
Above this again tier upon architectural tier of a dusking vault
Lit by a lonely wing, gliding small as snowflake and as silently.

VANESSA, VANESSA

Three roads were shadowy and the sky over.
One road was mine with many people marching far.
One road so solitary it seemed untrodden, a road alone.
The third was rutted, old with Time and tracks, the parent road.
And at the fork of the roads Two stood: one waiting,
The other looking and wondering, anxious how she might choose.

But the waiting one, this was I, knew
There was no choice to make, or if there were
It was already too late, for her mould was setting.
And it was in that shadowy land as if my hands reached out
Not once but twice, pleadingly: once with, ah, such desire
To bring her along my road; once with sterner zeal
To set her on that lone, that solitary second path.

Twice: but each time my hands went through and fell
As if through greylit nothing: where her breasts were, arms were,
All was as shadows, though from the waist down something shrank in fear.
And slowly along the third, the parent road, she went,
Shade fading within the shadows, lost to me, to herself,
To the world: lost and looking back.

NICK NICHOLLS

THE BONE AND THE FLOWER

I

Wound in the seed, the rose's tongue,
Among flowers, the chatter of light and shade,
Lights on the long pier out to sea,
Down there in the valley and on the beach,
Down there in the loam of soil and sea,
Darkness has flowered in the rose,
The bone and the flower are one.

Time's gullible shade has penetrated
Mud and matter. Material forms
Disperse. Lion is Greek for Xerxes.
Loam is salt for sea. Under
The towering pyramid and the mythogothic
  shades
Darkness has flowered into the shining rose,
The bone of the flower and the power of the
  bone
Are one rose clipped into the bell of peace.

II

Said the rose to the bone, I am death,
  Darkness of love and brightness of flower;
Said the rose to the bone, I am the breath
  Of the mute, infallible hour

When life is the dark rose of flesh
  And flesh is the bright flowering bone
And darkness and death are one incontestible mesh
  Bound to the seed and the loam

Gyration of life and bone and flower,
When the voice of the flesh in the darkness of bone
Is the light of the rose in the immemorial hour,
The immemorial hour of the death of the rose and the bone.

III

I am of light, said the bone
I am the crucial power,
Hardness of rock and stone
Brightness of flame and flower.

I am of fire, said the rose
Born to devour
Brightness of rock and stone
Hardness of flame and flower.

IV

But in the terror, the darkness of the coiled rose
The flowering penultimate power of the unborn rose
But in the dread, the unborn power of the flowering rose
Coiled in the dark flower, the dark power of the unborn dead.

V

Rose of silence, rose of death
Coiled in the darkness of tongue and breath
Rose of darkness, rose of fire
Coiled in the interminable, indestructible hour.

O paroxysmic power
Intercysmic bone of light,
Instrumental in the hour
Of dark and dark and light and light.

VI

Dark, dark, dark the power
  Of unwieldy magnificence in the breath
Dark, dark, dark the hour
  Of the intractable and encoiled breath.

Dark, dark, dark the flower's entanglements,
  The virulent rose, the flagellant power;
Dark the hour of the flower's entanglements,
  The sibilant rose, the insinuate power!

VII

As the rock to the flesh
As the bridge to the stream
Irrevócable the mesh
Of rock and dream

As the bone to the flower
As the wall to the garden
The innocent power
Of the rose will harden

VIII

Into the squat shape of the flower,
Into the lumbering rock,
One rose and reasonable power
To intone and shock

The litugry of brain and tower,
The dark, marmoreal shape
Of the squat flower in the squat brain,
The dark rose of the ape.

IX

Chaos of shadow and bone and flesh
Chaos of shadow and bone and rock
Surmounting the bone and the flesh and the
  shock
Wound in the dark irrigátory mesh

Of valley and shadow and stone and rock
Bound in the round of tower and clock
Of darkness wound in the heart of light
Bones on the hillside and bones out of sight

Chaos of rock and tower and hill
Gyration of bone and flower and rock
Bones in the valley and bones in the mill
Bound in the round of tower and clock.

X

I am birth, said the rose
  Seed of decay
I am light, said the bone
  Born each day.

I am power, said the bone
  Whiplash and tear
I am love, said the rose
  Hunger and fear.

I am life, said the bone
  Muscle and blood
I am death, said the rose
  Fire and flood.

XI

One light, one light, in bone and flower,
One periphrastic, impenetrable power,
One dark successive light, one weave
Of bone and flesh, one mute intolerable hour
When all is none, and all is power
And the violence of the rose, and all
The saintly flower, concupiscent with death,
The flowering bone, the flowering breath
In labour, one shape and season,
Rose of extinction and rebirth.

XII

So the rose and the bone were united in the dark peace of death,
And the dark shadow of the rock and the flesh was for ever erased,
And the memory of man once more took on the character of its birth
In the light of the testimony of the flesh, in the light of the bone, in the light of the indestructible rose.

D. J. O'SULLIVAN

DAWN IN INISHTRAHULL

The moon shines on the Isle of Inishtrahull,
Bejewelling nuptial-tinted herring-gull,
May-fly dancing in the balmy air,
And moth returning to its daylight lair.

A shoal of herring breaking out at sea
Sparkle like hoar-frost on an aspen tree,
Spindrift in the shaded rocky cleft,
And raised-beach quartz that the ice-ages left.

The droning beetles seek the crevassed walls
To dive into when hungry lapwing calls;
Earwigs, likewise, into earthed homes.
And red ants under scarred lichened stones.

An otter seeking rest on rock remote
Glistens with phosphorescence on his coat,
The snail *Arborum,* with its watery glue,
And bunch of pearlwort in a crystal dew.

The flaming sun ascends o'er Cantyre's Mull,
Flings out his arms, day breaks on Inishtrahull.

LATE EVENING

The pale sea-pinks are gymped with spray,
Thrown by the dancing breeze-swept tide;
And lichens yellow, silver-grey,
Adorn the scarred rocks beside.

Wee white-faced glabrous chickweeds hold
With threadlike rootlets to their beds,
Tall cats-ear flowering purest gold
Nods its several-branchéd heads.

The sunset-wheel illumes the sky
With spokes of stippled amber-light,
We hear a sentry curlew's cry;
The limestone cliffs glint ghostly white!

W. R. RODGERS

CHRIST WALKING ON THE WATER

Slowly, O so slowly, longing rose up
In the forenoon of his face, till only
A ringlet of fog lingered round his loins;
And fast he went down beaches all weeping
With weed, and waded out. Twelve tall waves
Sequent and equated, hollowed and followed.
O what a cock-eyed sea he walked on,
What poke-ends of foam, what elbowings
And lugubrious looks, what ebullient
And contumacious musics. Always there were
Hills and holes, pills and poles, a wavy wall
And bucking ribbon caterpillaring past
With glossy ease. And often, as he walked,
The slow curtains of swell swung open and showed,
Miles and miles away, the bottle-boat
Flung on one wavering frond of froth that fell
Knee-deep and heaved thigh-high. In his forward
  face
No cave of afterthought opened; to his ear
No bottom clamour climbed up; nothing blinked.
For he was the horizon, he the hub,
Both bone and flesh, finger and ring of all
This clangorous sea. Docile, at his toe's touch,
Each tottering dot stood roundaboutly calm
And jammed the following others fast as stone.
The ironical wave smoothed itself out
To meet him, and the mocking hollow
Hooped its back for his feet. A spine of light
Sniggered on the knobbly water, ahead.
But he like a lover, caught up,

Pushed past all wrigglings and remonstrances
And entered the rolling belly of the boat
That shuddered and lay still. And he lay there
Emptied of his errand, oozing still. Slowly
The misted mirror of his eyes grew clear
And cold, the bell of blood tolled lower,
And bright before his sight the ocean bared
And rolled its horrible bold eyeballs endlessly
In round rebuke. Looking over the edge
He shivered. Was this the way he had come?
Was that the one who came? The backward bowl
And all the bubble-pit that he had walked on
Burst like a plate into purposelessness.
All, all was gone, the fervour and the froth
Of confidence, and flat as water was
The sad and glassy round. Somewhere, then,
A tiny flute sounded, O so lonely.
A ring of birds rose up and wound away
Into nothingness. Beyond himself he saw
The settled steeples, and breathing beaches
Running with people. But he,
He was custodian to nothing now,
And boneless as an empty sleeve hung down.
Down from crowned noon to cambered evening
He fell, fell, from white to amber, till night
Slid over him like an eyelid. And he,
His knees drawn up, his head dropped deep,
Curled like a question-mark, asleep.

POEM

From my wind-blown book I look
Up and see the lazy rook
Rise and twist away,

And from every airy eave
The arrowy swallows wildly leave
And swoop as if in play.

Dark the daw with claw-wing sail
Swings at anchor in the gale,
And in the running grass
Daffodils nod and intervene
Like sud-flecks on a sea of green
Dissolving as they pass.

Mouldy and old the boulder walls
Wake in the sun and warm their polls
And wag aubrietia beards,
The snail-glaze of senility
Silvers each front, and backward they
Break wind and dree their weirds.

Bosoms of bloom that sob like moss
Beneath each jumpy breath, emboss
The bony orchard's breast;
And look, the leggy lilac-canes
Are varicosed with ivy veins
Of gravy coalesced.

There the hare, bound after bound,
Concertinas all the ground
As far as eye can spy it,
Like a fountain's dying spray
It falls in little frills away
Into a twitching quiet.

Still down the slow opposing slope
The intent ploughman draws his rope
Of parsimony fine,

Nor notices Icarus in his haste
Expend his spirit in a waste
Of aerobatic wine.

Icarus from his heady plane
Into depths of spinning brain
Bales out like a ball,
Pulls the ripcord, splits the sack
And lets the spilled silk splutter back
And speculative fall.

And hark, the lark sarcastic sings
To Icarus without his wings
Dawdling down the sky,
Indolent aeons have gone to make
Its gimlet bill, its song-gills' shake,
Its all-containing cry.

APOLLO AND DAPHNE

Look how her close defences laddered like
A stocking, knee to toe ran suddenly
In one lean stroke, flawed and flowed like wate
Crowding the tiny breach in some tall dyke
And zipping open a Zuyder Zee
Of privacy. What does it matter
If she lay passive and refused to strike?

For when the flying hare, her breast mud-beaten
Hears the hounds gain and give tongue greedily
A field away, and feels their huddled thud
Thundering and darkening the ground before her
How her breath leaves her, and her feet connive
And hungry eyes let go their hold of home,
And all her heart is lifted up from her,

No longer arguing, agreeing now
With her devoted and devouring fate;
And, floating out upon the wind, her cry
Circles the scene with careless quisling eye.

So this doomed woman, hounded and brought low,
Wheels round and meets her captor toe to toe
And face to face. Deep in the other's eyes
She sees herself, and smiles, a solemn mime
There in the mirror where her halves embrace
And consummate the marriage of the chase.

For, from that last and zero tower of Time,
Lifted above herself her heart can see
The self that followed and the self that fled
(Through all the long and roundabout of days),
Closing the circle irremediably
Of life and death, in one brief blinding gaze:
And in the awful night of pain long-drawn
Rises a conflagration of peace, a bloody dawn.

AN IRISH LAKE

There in the hard light
Dark birds, pink-footed, dab and pick
Among the addery roots and marrowy stones,
And the blown waves blink and hiccup at the lake's
Lip. A late bee blares and drones on inland
Into a cone-point of silence, and I
Lying at the rhododendron's foot
Look through five fingers' grille at the lake
Shaking, at the bare and backward plain, and
The running and bending hills that carry
Like a conveyor-belt the bright snail-line
Of clouds along the sky all day unendingly.

There, far from the slack noose of rumour
That tightens into choking fact, I relax
And sounds and sights and scents sail slowly by.
But suddenly, like delicate and tilted italics,
The upstanding birds stretch urgently away
Into the sky as suddenly grown grey.
Night rounds on Europe now. And I must go.
Before its hostile faces peer and pour
Over the mind's rim enveloping me,
And my so-frightened thoughts dart here and there
Like trout among their grim stony gazes.

STORMY DAY

O look how the loops and balloons of bloom
Bobbing on long strings from the finger-ends
And knuckles of the lurching cherry-tree
Heap and hug, elbow and part, this wild day,
Like a careless carillon cavorting;
And the beaded whips of the beeches splay
And dip like anchored weed round a drowned rock,
And hovering effortlessly the rooks
Hang on the wind's effrontery as if
On hooks, then loose their hold and slide away
Like sleet sidewards down the warm swimming
  sweep
Of wind. O it is a lovely time when
Out of the sunk and rigid sumps of thought
Our hearts rise and race with new sounds and sights
And signs, tingling delightedly at the sting
And crunch of springless carts on gritty roads,
The caught kite dangling in the skinny wires,
The swipe of a swallow across the eyes,
Striped awnings stretched on lawns. New things
  surprise

And stop us everywhere. In the parks
The fountains scoop and flower like rockets
Over the oval ponds whose even skin
Is pocked and goosefleshed by their niggling rain
That frocks a naked core of statuary.
And at jetty's jut, roped and ripe for hire,
The yellow boats lie yielding and lolling,
Jilted and jolted like jellies. But look!
There! Do you see, crucified on palings,
Motionless news-posters announcing
That now the frozen armies melt and meet
And smash? Go home now, for, try as you may
You will not shake off that fact to-day.
Behind you limps that dog with tarry paw,
As behind him, perfectly timed, follows
The dumb shadow that mimes him all the way

IRELAND

O these lakes and all gills that live in them,
These acres and all legs that walk on them,
These tall winds and all wings that cling to them,
Are part and parcel of me, bit and bundle,
Thumb and thimble. Them I am, but none more
Than the mountains of Mourne that turn and
  trundle
Roundly like slow coils of oil along the shore
Of Down and on inland. When I begin
To draw my memory's nets and outlines in,
Then through its measured mesh escapes the fuss
And fluster of all finicky things.
Of the Mournes I remember most the mist,
The grey granite goosefleshed, the minute
And blazing parachutes of fuchsia, and us
Listening to the tiny clustered clinks

Of little chisels tinkling tirelessly
On stone, like a drip of birds' beaks picking
Rapidly at scattered grain. I think of those
Wet sodden days when we, for miles and miles,
Steadily padded the slow sponge of turf
That squealed and squelched between our bared toes;
Or on airy ridge, urgent and agile, ran,
A chain of jigging figures on the sky-line;
Or, skilfully in file, followed, tricking
The loops of hairy bramble in our path,
Poking in undergrowth and picking
The bitter berries that prickle the springs
Of the dark mouth. There was Bloody River
Where the granite pickles bristled and blazed, and
Ebullient water bellied over
Boulders with the sweep of a bell's shoulders,
And pancaked out in pools: Drinihilla
Where the gales smoothed and glued back the
    eyelids:
The granite river that is called Kilkeel,
Whose beds were clean and gritty like oatmeal:
And Commedagh in whose high summer heat
Nothing stirred, only the shimmering bleat
Of sheep; and we, as we sat and chattered,
Marked the motionless shine of falls far-off
On Binyon, and nothing at all mattered:
And Legawherry so soft and grassy,
Where the white scuts lazily scattered,
And never in their remotest burrows
Did ferret-fear come closely after them:
Slieve-na-brock and its long pigtail trickles
That hung down the bald rocks, reaching to
The glossy backs of the bracken. And Donard
Where, high over all hanging, the strong hawk
Held in his eyes whole kingdoms, sources, seas,
And in his foot-hooks felt all things wriggling

Like the single string of river niggling
Among the enormous mountain bottoms.
Bearnagh and Lamigan and Chimney-Rock,
Spelga, Pulgarve and Cove—all these names lie
Silently in my grass-grown memory,
Each one bright and steady as a frog's eye;
But touch it and it leaps, leaps like a bead
Of mercury that breaks and scatters
Suddenly in a thousand shining strings
And running spools and ever-dwindling rings
Round the mind's bowl, till at last all drop,
Lumped and leaden again, to one full stop.

SUMMER HOLIDAYS

New every morning now the clerk docks off
Yesterday's desk-date, jerks back the needle
On duty's disc, and noses and slides on
Round the ingrowing ring and exact track
Of old tactics till the day's contracting
Circle ends, and suddenly the idle needle
Skids wildly into zigzag freedom
And tidy tailspin, the clerk knocks off
Abruptly, buttoning up his coat.

And later, no doubt, you will see him
Nosing and sliding in orderly line
Into pin-lighted cinema, being led
Alertly to allotted seat of ease,
Relaxing with eyes like asterisks,
Or note him standing in stadium rind,
Waiting for joy to be unconfined, wanting
The electric hare let loose to recapture
Its first fine careless rapture.

Even here at the day's convenient halt
And within its convolvulus ring
He has his own hugged track, his strangling string
Of ingrained act, his railed and ready ease;
And coiled in this roundabout and tail-chase
Of private scope and escape is ever
The spin of flesh on the spindle of bone
Concentrating all, with its brute ambitions,
Its acute and terrible attritions.

But few look up to see or consider
This, the slack and screw of their happiness,
The economic claw, the heart's own flaw,
The ambient of mixed routine and rout,
Few look, except to the standing desk-date
(Their only shoremark) that notes and notches
Time's indivisibly flowing miles,
That recognizes the returning tide,
That remembers the arriving traveller.

New every morning through a thousand streets
Life siphons into offices, and worms
Into old workings, yet the entombed man
Waiting behind the walled weeks hears always
The deliberate taps of time loudening
And the rescuing days drawing nearer,
Till at last hope opens and the gloom
Gapes like a tomb about him—holiday hands
Beckon him from far lands, urge his escape.

So out of pent city and inland pit
They nose and slide by easy rut and rail
To distant sea-edge, spreading boldly
On sand-dunes, or lolling on piers
(The leash-ends of land),

Or, in pairs, pacing slowly, posing as idlers
Till the last hill hides
Them, and they hurry deliberately
On to the Land's End and hilt's halt of heart's
desire.

Longing to skip over the edge of scope
They look out all day at the far islands,
Or scan with glass the slipping distances
To where, bold in some enormous valley,
Walled and bottomed by the swinging water,
The cormorant squats; or between tide-lines
They march for miles searching for shells, leaping
Back when the swan-neck wave pours down and
pounds
Out to yellow hissing beaks at their feet.

Here in these strange places no memory
Arrests and edits the running reel
Of their eager extravagant acts, fear
Lays no detaining or determining hand
On them, the backward light of precedent
No longer faces them with dutiful shadows
—Frolicking lives that at a finger's touch
Will curl like worms into a stiff conceit
And dead front of frightened consciousness.

Along the valley roads some roll in cars,
Looking for life in sky-lines, or in bars,
Mustered in bus on mystery trip they cheer
As the chartered miles gape before them,
And zip obediently behind them,
Their fixed stare clattering like a stick
Across the sliding face and fence of fields
To the full stop where they interrogate
The great man's birthplace, or the rebel's grave.

Through bright gaps these sudden strangers snapshot
The slipshod landscape, and depart content.
But, coming home in the bare evening,
Memory on the mind's horizon edge
Like lightning prickles and flashes, and Care
Like caterpillar in curled leaf shrinks the heart,
For still the thread and threat of memory
Runs through these strange places and faces and
Jerks back the jumping beads of time and space.

And still from frugal bungalow and fig-leaf tent
The stockbroker, the stonebreaker, and the candle-
  stick-maker
Trot into shop for morning newspaper,
Afraid to let the world go by without
Accommodating eye, anxious to acquaint
And equate their happiness with all
Unbalancing happenings, helplessly
Eager to follow the involving game
Of territorial noughts and crosses.

And still each night from alp and valley lap,
From all dividing individual aims
Life spokes into the town's sociable hub,
Where, under confetti-freckle of lights,
The girls in banana-bright bandanas
Parade down prickly lanes and lines of eyes;
Others round fun-stand wait the rocket-flash
Of wit on upturned faces, or applaud
The seal-like vocalist balancing one last note on
  voice-tip.

Far out on the wavering water they see
The pointed ship probe on to express end,
While they freely to-night at the slack edge
Of the vehement sea of affairs sit

And saunter; soon all must enter
That stiff and teeming centre, to-morrow
Each homing heart released by time-table
Springs dove-like back to office ark and task, gives
One last elastic look and snaps away.

Away from outer rout to inner rut
And ironed route, away from the wild
And unwalled waste of wish, the zigzag tracks,
The wilful freaks and fractures of habit,
The staccato acts of insurrection,
The guilty bed, the naked bathe, the night
Annexed from niggard eyes by drunkenness,
The lonely climb at dawn, all the jerky
Gap-toothed gamut of places and spaces.

Away from these eccentric ends to the city's
Centripetal calm and planetary core
Of custom and corporate act, away
To private lawns and privet lanes
With pilot kerbs and polite drains,
Day's slick pay-lines, night's slack play-pens,
Where we are ticketed and trickled into
Stalls, and turnstiled into galleries and grades
And apt groups, like pebbles that elbow and
Rub shiny shoulders on a narrow beach.

—Thus on the round and turning stage of flesh
We present to you the usual act,
Rut and Rout, alias Butt and Rebut,
Alias Leash and Release, the magpie pair
In their bitter backbiting, ball-bouncing,
And reciprocating patter. No doubt
You have seen it before, for it is
The same yesterday, to-day, and for ever,
Showing at all houses and theatres,
The skeleton of all our furbished plays.

For not by gradual stealthy steps do we
Move onwards to a plotted destiny,
But between antinomies we are stretched
And pent, and catapulted to new ends
And angry issues. Note, now, how in us
Each thing resists and buoys its opposite,
Goodness is foreskinned and frisked by Evil,
And Violence advances Reason's forces,
Cruelty recruits Kindness, and titan
Dictators tickle tomtit democrats.

And Faith beats down the enemy's last gate,
But listless then within resistless halls
Dies of its enemy's death; thus do you see
The saw-toothed graph drawn daily, inking
The in-and-out of action, linking rut and rout,
But few look up to know, few seek to master
These seesaw forces until disaster
Breaks the pithless sticks of apathy, and then
Through gaps of anger heady droves will hurry
And into panic-traps hot hooves will huddle.

And what will be left of us then but our faces
In albums, our names on war's memorials,
Our number on old disc picked up by peasant?
History's putty shapes, pitied or praised
According to public mode or private mood,
We have done it ourselves and need expect
No less, for the music goes round and round
In the old rings, new every morning,
The spin of flesh on the spindle of bone
Concentrating all, with its brute ambitions,
Its acute and terrible attritions.

BLANAID SALKELD

EVASION

The old woman has forgotten her face:
a chance mirror met, to avoid disgrace
she blinks her glance with lightning wit;
no recognition reflects in it.

The maid at the dresser drops the delph
as someone enters; she is all thumbs—
but the old woman holds on to herself,
sucking her gums.

If I didn't shrink—I am so diminished,
the old one thinks, I feel cold shy
of strange members that seem never finished
casting off and losing that thing was I:
she turns objective, for shame—in case
she might have to acknowledge her latest face.

THEORY

Art for art's sake—death for death's sake:
Each were a similar mistake.
Man dies for freedom—principle—plain love.
Death or impersonal art is not enough.
That dubious sudden jerk to Heaven or
Hell. . . .
Art that endows posterity: ah, well,
Love scarcely can go further than to bequeathe
Joy to mankind grouped painfully beneath—

When love lifts rhythmic wings, a blissful
spirit,
Above its dear heirs, happy to inherit
Fruits of old temporal toil, harsh discipline.
Never has there been written a lasting line
But out of love. Those clear-devised ambitions,
That greed, that envy: they are small seditions
Against the immortal soul's desire through
rhyme,
Colour and note to vibrate still in time.
Lord, I have loved: forgive that I have sinned.
The poet's tears are cherished by the wind.
His far flung cry may dim a star, long after
The critic's scorn is dumb and his false
laughter.

GEOFFREY TAYLOR

ST. MAELRUAN'S CHURCH

Through the thin winter bareness of the wood
Each time one crossed this field there the church
  stood,
In ill-proportioned elegance, eye-plain:
But look, before the summer leaves again
In say a fortnight's time or thereabouts—
Depending on the weather—blot it out,
How, shadow-laced by elm-tree's powder-green.
Grace grows enhanced till grace alone is seen.
So viewed, the point of view will underline
Whatever of genius eighteen-twenty-nine
Conferred on architect Semple, which was not
At other times, from anywhere, a lot.

  Like sugar-piping on a limestone cake
He placed those little pinnacles to break
His elevation's bulk, which else had been
Only if not significant, not mean.
(Semple had topped them all with well-carved stones
Removed last year, replaced by meagre cones.)
For when, as workman worthy of his hire,
He raised the natural question of a spire,
He found this rich though rural congregation
Had not the smallest spiral aspiration,
Reckoned that spires went hand in glove with pence
Implying hand in pocket—deeper; hence
The vestry had to voice the rational view
That the adjacent ruined tower would do,
Repointed and rebattlemented, well
Or well enough to hang their tinkling bell.

So Semple's genius—talent—either way—
Hadn't exactly what you'd call fair play.
Yet even so, he did create a thing
Of almost beauty, seen from this field, in spring.

BOATHAVEN, Co. MAYO

That house, a stone's throw from the shell-strewn
shore,
Now nearly swallowed by encroaching trees
That creep upon it from the hill behind,
Itself a shell like any of these, gaping
And broken but still beautiful, was built
By Smuggler Jordan in seventeen-twenty or so.

Gable and wings toward the crumpled sea,
With vacant door and window, yet look out
Through unkempt hair of undergrowth—the door
And lower windows all but blocked by nettles—
In the spare sunlight and tart air of autumn.
What once were lawns remain like lawn, kept clipt
By sandhill-warrened rabbits, to high tide;
While of the garden, one exotic fig-tree
Still struggles strangled by black-fruited brambles.

Then who on earth was Jordan? I don't know.
Only his name survives among the peasantry.
English perhaps, a bit rough-tongued no doubt;
He may have had a palate for French wine
Or brandy landed on this awkward coast
Too intricate for revenue men to watch;
But he had certainly an eye for building,
Or else employed an architect who had.

So, granted an eye for a right elevation,
A nice taste too in moulding and stuccoed brick,
Let me suppose he judged a face and figure,
Manner and heart, with justice; had in fact
A wife who'd grace the landscape and the house;
Who'd read Matt Prior and not forget her prayers;
Cold-curved, demure, and coyly courteous
At picnics or when company would dine;
Coiled and familiar in her feather bed;
High-breasted and bright-eyed—a girl for whom
It might have been delight, with contraband
Of coarser kind, to land French silks and ribands.

One idly speculates, because one must
People a place—if only to complete
The picture for a sentiment.
However,
Now all that's left after two hundred years—
A name and this façade that keeps a name
Still faintly in men's memory—will go;
For there's enough cut stone in coping and lintel
Still to call forth a natural cupidity
In any native who's a byre to build.

A GIRL RENOUNCES THE CONVENT

This I will give, all this, all this. Consider,
Held for a moment, how untoiling grows—
No ethic auctioned to the highest bidder—
That unheraldic lily, that wild rose.
This I will give; a gift I give; not trading
Higgle on haggle all my this for that
In-fancy-fashioned future of unfading;
Driving a bargain, offering tit for tat.

Lily and rose; gold hair, red lips, red nipples—
Emblems of Essence in which death and birth
Are equal waves (themselves fun-freckled ripples),
These life to life I give, and with what mirth
I see you come, tottering antique to-morrows,
Toothless and fringed about with crowsfoot furrows.

HOUSE AND GARDEN

The house ten years back if not new
Was neatly pointed; and there grew
Pruned or prinked or in prim order,
Square or circle, bed or border,
Cabbages in formal row
And every flower that care can grow.
But in lapsed years, unseen, unheard,
Gradual carelessness occurred
By change of hand or heart or head.
Now nettle and cow-parsley spread
From flowerbed to flowerbed;
And myriad-fingered ivy picks
The plaster bond between the bricks.
Oh nettled shade, umbel of umbels,
Wet wall that under ivy crumbles—
What lack they beauty, heaven knows,
That had trim brickwork and bright rose?—
By right return outlasting these
Uneasy ephemerides.

BRUCE WILLIAMSON

FOR M——

It is not easy to be less than lovers,
I think it is simpler far
To catch the wind's bridle,
Thrust up and ride between the cheering
trees
Bank upon bank of leafy throatiness,
Fulfilling once again
What the sun has promised for us
Of partnership and pain.
Each year attends our downfall
And yet does something more
Than shift a subsoil,
Grant an acre less
To this poor family.
The nursery's kingdom now stands out of
doors
The golliwog reigns in terror on the hill
And shakes his startled locks against the sky.
Now is the time to thank
Our stars for their exciting twist and curl.
Though drunken in their cradles
They dare better
To settle finally for ever
What cut our veins and jerked our feet away.

Should the hawk and the oyster mate
Surprise would not halt us,
The slighting and chiding of lovers
Call no correction.

We know too well that those in partnership
Break down each other's health.
Why should we die this way,
Tense as a drill of light on the open sea,
We who had ankles and poise
And fists to crack nuts in,
We who as children understood cruelty?
Long ago in a big house they danced
And pair by pair they left me.
But the woman I could not touch
Stayed by the fire.
Oh, when at last I slept,
Who was I to know
She was the only one who kept
Her promise and her way of speaking.
This is my question: Was she the one
Who ran, her head above the cornstalks,
  laughing,
When she was twelve?
Who said: Is it true we must bear it
This vast undoing of hate?
Yes, then as children
We must have teased and chattered in the sun
The drift and catch of the wind
Came to us easily,
Came to us then.

NOW I MUST TRAVEL

Now I must travel
The circuit of her sorrow
Plead with myself for grief
And out of love pretend
Still to desire summer.

Last franchise of her day,
Her will and her sweet contagion,
I have taken from her
And left her to imagine
What befell the venturing river,
The frothing orchard and the creaking wood;
How, in the end, it all came out as loss,
The bloom and the bounty.
Then I had told her
Time was a clock on the rainbow
And she my dear surmised
How lost the dying were
Who had not love to think of
As they fussed and died.
All of us moving to each other's arms
Will die indeed,
But none remember then,
Faced with the greatest action in their lives,
Whose arms they moved to.
So I would fondly keep
Untried what she believed.
The wounded ponder
Why they move no closer
And the moon shapes up,
Newly or lately pruned,
Still frigid from eclipse.
If I could take and tie
The apron of the sky
Around my scorn and shame
I would as like as not live on
Unthinking of her name.
In the oasis of our own tall shadows
Imperilled yet we kissed,
And in the pensive welter of her mouth
All crops were clover.
Her eyes alone made sense

Of the cities tumbling closer
In companionate neurosis.
And it would have been my vice
Had I in love belied her
And thought about her twice.
Set on a fair wing,
I hope she knows her way
And which are the punished waters
That never reach the sea.
And I who suffered nothing,
Will in the end die hardest.
Fraught then of autumn or of spring,
Fetched up with a hollow throat
Too crackleboned to sing.
For I who suffered nothing,
Will in the end die hardest.

SACRED STONE

Stone and rock stand in varied sculpture,
Casting chill haloes of prehistory in the baptismal air.
The deep sockets of caves send their lonely stare
Across the purling sea, the ever enriching sepulture.
Monoliths lean from the hammers of the wind.
In chivvying circles the gulls fly blind.

Set adrift by hooks of cloud, the mountains float
Above the storm. On Haughmond Hill
A brown douche of leaves washes the still
Sweet earth, setting a patched russet coat
Across the evening's dusky, rippling shoulders.
The river's savage wrist lathers the gleaming boulders
But where is the wilderness of stone, the compromise

Of faith with endeavour? Like a plague wind from an
Arab port
Desire leaves us listless, impressed in the terrible fort
Where we are past action, intent on defection and lies.
Love is put by, and the granulated breath
Of the sirocco whips us in the first agony of death.

Pyramid, Druid's circle, Devil's chair . . . all sacred
stone
Entombs the wilderness. We stumble among the graves,
Trying to find whose sacrifice it is that saves
Our godhead. But these headstones are our own.
Waves break on the strand of life, each tide flows a
little beyond
The other, and takes new treasures to bond.

MARLAY

The trees spend themselves in striving
To the enchanted sky. The snow hangs on branches
Like tattered sails after a storm's abating.
As I walk through the park, I feel them arriving
Out of the bright clear night, their ocean without horizon,
Beyond the lissom moment of the heart's contriving.
Under its warp of snow
Marlay lies still as a needle
Devoted to a point. I go
Between the trees. I am the founder
Of a free world. I am at liberty
To choose my governors, and I choose them here,
Where the owl's eyes grow rounder
With gazing on white acres, and the lights
Of the revelling ice.

The flawless haunches of snow encircle me.
These cool thighs caught in the act of love, will not deny
Their lover, but will caress my stumbling blood
Into ascension, into that lonely mystery
Of union. It is wrong that there should be strangers
Who only desire each other's strangeness, who feel no
common history.
The shadows come around
Like silky animals that trail
Their great ears on the ground.
Ivory flails of moonlight beat
Above the absent crops,
Above next summer's granary.
The air is full of the tread of swollen feet
Too tired to march or trip,
Too tired to stop.

Armoured in moonlight too, the spires stand,
Rising all over Dublin. Man's frozen appetites ascend
No higher than his wish for comradeship.
Thousands of sore and twisted backs, thousands of wills
unmanned
By simple needs, rest quiet without hope or succour.
The steeples point the fingers of a cold admonitory hand
Mist floats across the rooftops
Like a sigh never to be spent.
It is the harsh breath that stops
The sound of innocence in the throat,
Forbids its proclamation, forbids
Our recognition and our trust
And sets a dark and iron-cold moat
Between us all.